Big
Knitting

Big Knitting

Sophie Britten

Martingale®
& COMPANY

Martingale & Company
20205 144th Avenue NE
Woodinville, WA 98072-8478 USA
www.martingale-pub.com

First published in the USA by Martingale & Company.

ISBN 1-56477-617-4

Senior Editor: Clare Sayer
Production: Hazel Kirkman
Design: Sue Rose
Photographer: Shona Wood
Editorial Direction: Rosemary Wilkinson

10 09 08 07 06 05   8 7 6 5 4 3 2 1

Reproduction by Pica Digital PTE Ltd, Singapore
Printed and bound by Times Offset (M) Sdn. Bhd., Malaysia

Contents

Introduction

In recent years, knitting has seen an exciting resurgence in popularity and a whole new generation of knitters is springing up. However, a growing number of knitters simply don't have time to spend all winter working on a complicated Fair Isle sweater. Instead they want to be able to create beautiful garments in bright colors and gorgeous yarns quickly for instantly wearable results. The good news is that knitting has never been quicker or easier and this book is a celebration of the great variety of the big and beautiful yarns now widely available, and the wonderful things that can be created on large needles.

This book contains 19 skill-rated patterns for sweaters, cardigans and shawls and the emphasis is firmly on projects that can be achieved in a weekend, using simple yet effective techniques.

For the learner knitter, the first part of the book covers all the basics and teaches you everything you will need to know to follow any of the patterns. Most patterns are easy enough for a beginner, with some more challenging pieces for the more experienced knitter. Or if you want to make something a bit different, there is some useful information on designing your own sweater at the beginning of the book which will tell you everything you need to know to create your own designs.

So whatever your taste or style, get out your giant needles and start creating fantastic garments. I hope you enjoy making the projects as much as I have enjoyed designing them.

Getting started

The great thing about knitting is that you need very little equipment to get going – just choose your yarn and needles and off you go!

NEEDLES

Knitting needles are available in aluminum, plastic and wood, although the larger sizes are only made in plastic and wood, as they are lighter and easier to hold.

Most yarns carry recommendations for needle sizes on the ball band, but generally speaking, thick yarns are knitted using large needles and thinner yarns with small ones. This produces a fabric that is neither too tight nor too loose. The thicker the needle, the larger the stitch and the more quickly your work will progress.

Knitting needles do vary in length, and for the projects in this book, where you will often be working on fairly wide fabric, the longer the better, as you may not have the option of using circular needles to carry stitches. Circular and double-pointed needles are not as readily available in the needle sizes used here.

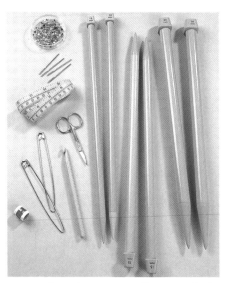

Apart from knitting needles, very little extra equipment is needed.

OTHER USEFUL EQUIPMENT

Crochet hooks These are very useful for picking up dropped stitches. You can also use them for binding off, creating edges, joining seams and adding tassels.

Stitch holder This keeps stitches that you are not using in place – for example, at the neck where you are planning to add a neckband once all the pieces have been completed. You could also use a spare needle for this.

Point protectors These will stop stitches from falling off, and also protect the point of the needle.

Tapestry needles These blunt-ended needles are used for joining seams as they won't split the yarn.

Tape measure An essential item, as you will often need to measure your work.

Small sharp scissors Essential for cutting yarn.

Row counter Helps you keep track of stitches and rows completed.

Pins Use long pins with large heads for pinning pieces together that are ready for sewing.

YARNS

Recent years have seen a proliferation in multicolored, textured and super-chunky yarns and there is now a dazzling array of beautiful yarns to choose from. These include synthetic and synthetic mix yarns, as well as traditional natural fibers such as wool and cotton. Each type of yarn has a different look and quality and some may be more suited to certain projects than others. This book uses some of the thickest available yarns, which are knitted on large needles. This makes for fewer, bigger stitches, and garments that can be knitted up in no time.

Wool This is a natural yarn made from sheep fleece. It is warm, elastic and long lasting.

Cotton Less elastic than wool, but cooler to wear. It is also easy to wash and strong.

Mohair Known for its loft (fluffiness), this is the wool from an Angora goat. The long silky fibers make it very warm.

Angora Like mohair, but softer. It is made from the hair of the Angora rabbit.

KNITTING NEEDLE CONVERSION TABLE

METRIC	BRITISH	AMERICAN
8 mm	0	11
9 mm	00	13
10 mm	000	15
12 mm		17
15 mm		19
20 mm		36
25 mm		50

A huge range of chunky yarns is now available.

Alpaca Less fluffy than mohair and angora, it is made from the hair of a llama-like animal. It is very soft and can be used as a cheaper substitute for cashmere.

Cashmere Made from the very fine downy hair of a particular Asian goat, cashmere is hard to obtain and therefore very expensive. It is the softest and most luxurious of wools.

Chenille A velvety yarn made of tufts of cotton and synthetic yarn.

Fur The fur used in this book is a mix of wool and mohair strands attached to a narrow band that when knitted gives the fluffy effect of fur.

CHOOSING YARNS

To ensure your garment appears the same as in the pattern, you should use the yarn that the pattern recommends. If you cannot find the same yarn, choose one of a similar weight and type and knit a sample to check the gauge and appearance. When choosing yarn check the ball band for the dye lot number and make sure you buy balls with the same number. The number represents a specific dye bath and the color of each may differ slightly.

Never underestimate how much yarn you will need. It is better to have too much and return the surplus to the shop once you have completed your garment than to run out.

CARE AND WASHING INSTRUCTIONS

Care instructions should be given on the ball band, however where there is none, it is a good idea to wash a knitted sample first.

Wool Wash in cold or lukewarm water with a mild detergent, gently pressing the fabric. Do not pull or twist the garment. Rinse well several times until the water runs clear, then carefully lift the garment and squeeze out the water gently. Roll in a towel, and squeeze to absorb as much moisture as possible. To dry, lay the article on a dry towel on a flat surface, reshape, and leave.

Cottons and synthetics These can be machine-washed, but you should check the ball band for washing instructions first, and if in doubt, hand wash. Set the machine to a delicate cycle with warm or cold water and dry on a low heat.

TAKING MEASUREMENTS

Measurements for garments are based on body size, plus allowance for ease. In general, using big needles and chunky yarn creates a stretchy fabric, so the garments will have a lot more ease than their flat measurement indicates. However, you can reduce the number of stitches if you wish the garment to be smaller or narrower.

Check your size by taking your measurements for bust, hips and inside sleeve length (from just below the armpit to the wrist) to see which size garment you should make.

TIP

Wool is prone to felting when washed in hot soapy water. This causes the fibers to become meshed and tangled and the fabric to shrink. To avoid felting, use cool water and handle the fabric gently.

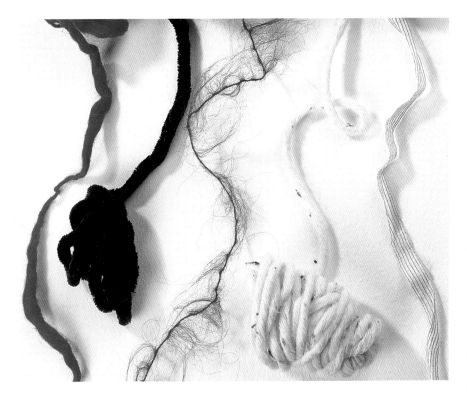

The yarns used in this book vary from textured wools to fluffy mohair.

Alternatively, you can measure an existing garment that you know to be a good fit.

Before you start a pattern, clearly mark which size you are going to make and highlight instructions for that size throughout the pattern. This will make it much easier to read.

FOLLOWING INSTRUCTIONS

Knitting patterns use special terminology that is often abbreviated or shown as symbols on a chart. All the patterns in the book use the standard abbreviations throughout (see right). Each pattern is broken up into clearly labelled parts indicating which piece of the garment you are working on.

Where there is a recurring instruction, the pattern to be repeated is shown with an asterisk before and after, e.g. *k1, p1* repeat pattern from * until last stitch.

TIP

To keep the gauge of a garment consistent, keep some scrap knitting on hand to warm up on each time you pick up your knitting.

ABBREVIATIONS

These are the abbreviations that are used in this book to make it quicker and easier to follow the pattern. It is not an exhaustive list, and you may find some of these terms abbreviated differently elsewhere.

alt	alternate
beg	begin(ning)
cm	centimeters
cont	continue
dec	decreas(e)(ing)
foll	following
g st	garter stitch (every row is knitted)
in.	inches
inc	increas(e)(ing)
k	knit
k2tog	knit two stitches together
p	purl
p2tog	purl two stitches together
patt	pattern
psso	pass slipped stitch over
rem	remain(ing)
rep	repeat
RS	right side
sl	slip a stitch from left needle to right
sl, k1, psso	slip 1, knit 1, pass slipped stitch over the knitted one
st(s)	stitch(es)
St st	stockinette stitch (knitted side is right side)
tbl	through back of loop
tog	together
WS	wrong side
yf	yarn forward to make a stitch
YO	yarn over needle

GAUGE

This is the number of rows and stitches per inch (centimeter), usually measured over a 4 in. (10 cm) square. The gauge will determine the size of the finished garment. The correct gauge is given at the beginning of each pattern. Knit a swatch using the recommended yarn and needles to make sure you are working to the correct gauge. If your work is too loose, choose a needle that is one size smaller. Similarly, if it is too tight, choose a needle the next size up. It is really important to spend a little time checking your gauge; it is not worth knitting something the wrong size.

Consistent tension is important for knitting even fabric. You should be able to knit easily into each stitch, but without leaving gaps. The advantage of working with chunky and variable-width yarns is that minor inconsistencies won't spoil the overall look.

To check your gauge, knit a sample about 6 in. (15 cm) square. Lay the piece flat on a cloth-covered level surface and pin the sample to the cloth without stretching it. Using a rigid tape measure or ruler, measure 4 in. (10 cm), mark with pins and count the number of stitches between the pins.

Checking the gauge of a swatch.

How to knit

The patterns in this book use only basic stitches and techniques but once you have mastered them you will be knitting in no time. There are several different ways of holding the needles and yarn and of casting on and knitting — use whichever feels more comfortable for you.

HOLDING THE NEEDLES AND YARN (right-handed method)

The tension and feed of the yarn is controlled with the right hand. Wrap the yarn around your little finger, and hold the yarn in your right hand as shown so that the yarn is about 2 in. (5 cm) from the work (A). The needle in your left hand will hold the stitches at the beginning of each row.

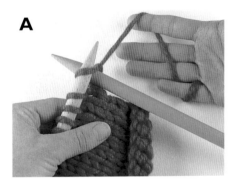

A

HOLDING THE NEEDLES AND YARN (Continental or left-handed method)

In continental or left-handed knitting, the yarn is controlled with the left

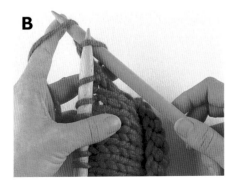

B

hand. The yarn is wrapped around the left index finger as shown and held extended about 2 in. (5 cm) away from the work (B).

CASTING ON

This is the method of getting stitches onto the needle so that you can start to knit.

Again, there are a number of different methods of casting on, but we will concentrate on the most popular methods, knitting on and the thumb method.

It is important to cast on evenly and not too tight, as this will form the first row that you will knit into. If your stitches are not even, it is worth doing them again.

Knitting on uses the same technique as the basic knit stitch and creates a soft and elastic edge. Start by making a slipknot. To do this, make a loop, and with the tip of the needle, make another loop and draw it through the first loop (C) and tighten, pulling the knot close to the needle.

C

With the slip knot on your left needle, insert the right needle into the front of the loop from left to right, wrap the yarn around the needle from right to left, under and over the needle.

With the right needle, draw through the loop you have just made towards you. You will now have a loop on the right needle. Transfer this

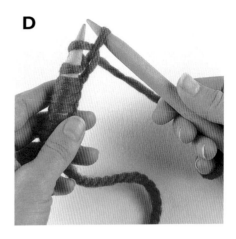

D

back onto the left needle, without twisting it (D). Repeat the process, inserting the right needle from left to right of the new stitch you have just made. This method of casting on is suitable for increasing the width of the fabric at one side.

Casting on purlwise

Some patterns may require you to cast on purlwise, for example the Batwing sleeve sweater, page 30. With the yarn held in front of the work, insert the right needle into the stitch from back to front and right to left. Wrap the yarn around the needle in a counterclockwise motion and draw through a loop. Transfer the new stitch back onto the left needle.

CASTING ON USING THE THUMB METHOD

This method of casting on is very quick and creates a flexible edge, although care should be taken not to make it too tight, otherwise it will be hard to knit the first row into it.

Unlike knitting on, you will be working towards the ball of yarn, so you will need to unravel as much as you think you need to cast on all the stitches. It is better to overestimate than to run out of yarn before you have finished casting on, as you can use a long tail for sewing seams.

English (right-handed) method

This method uses just one needle. Make a slipstitch on the needle. Hold the needle in your right hand. The yarn tail goes from the needle around your left thumb clockwise, and the tail end of the yarn is held tightly in the palm of your left hand. The yarn from the ball is controlled by your right index finger.

Twist your left thumb so the back of it faces you and insert the right needle from front to back of the loop made around your thumb. Wrap the yarn from the ball under and over the needle (E), draw through a loop, let the loop on your thumb slide off and pull the stitch reasonably, but not too tight.

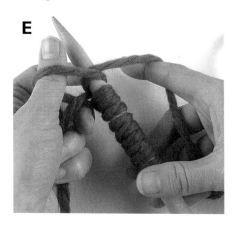

Continental (left-handed) method

Using this method, the yarn is held and controlled in the left hand, so in order to cast on using the thumb method, both the yarn tail and yarn from the ball are held in the left hand.

This method uses just one needle. Make a slipstitch on the needle. Hold the needle in your right hand. The yarn tail goes from the needle around your left thumb from back to front and the tail end of the yarn is held tightly in your palm. The yarn from the ball is controlled with your left index finger.

Twist your thumb so the back of it faces you and insert the right needle from front to back of the loop made round your thumb. With your left index finger, wrap the yarn from the

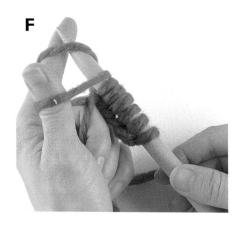

ball under and over the needle (F), draw through a loop, let the loop on your thumb slide off and pull the stitch reasonably (but not too) tight.

BASIC STITCHES

The most basic stitch of all is the knit stitch. It is a very similar process to casting on.

Knit stitch (right-handed method)

Once you have cast on the number of stitches you require, insert the right needle into the first stitch on the left needle from left to right and front to back. You will be holding the yarn behind the work. Now with the right index finger take the yarn under the needle (from right to left) and over the top of it (G). Draw the loop towards you through the stitch, and as you do this, push the original stitch on the left needle towards the tip of the needle, and let it slide off. You will now have one knit stitch on the right needle. Knitting every stitch and every row creates garter stitch.

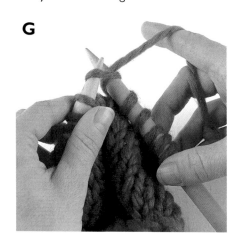

TIP

Keep the stitches on the left needle no more than an inch from the tip, using the fingers of your left hand to push the stitches forward. With your right hand, push back the stitches you have just made on the right needle.

Knit stitch (Continental or left-handed method)

Controlling the yarn with your left index finger, extend the yarn behind the left needle; insert the right needle into the first stitch on the left needle from left to right and front to back. Twist the right needle under the feed of the yarn from the index finger (H) and draw through a loop. Push the stitch off the tip of the left needle. You will now have one knit stitch on the right needle.

Purl stitch (right-handed method)

Purl stitch is the reverse of the knit stitch. If you were to purl every row, you would produce the same result as if you had worked in knit stitch.

With the yarn now in front of the work, insert your right needle into the first loop on the left needle from right to left (I). With your right index finger, move the yarn in a counterclockwise motion over the front of the needle, underneath and over again. Draw through the loop, pushing the right needle away from you whilst pushing the stitch on the left needle towards the tip and letting

I

it slide off. You will now have one purl stitch on the right needle.

Purl stitch (Continental or left-handed method)

Controlling the yarn with your left index finger, extend the yarn in front of the left needle; insert the right

J

needle into the first stitch on the left needle from right to left and back to front (J). Push the needle back through the stitch and draw through a loop. Push the stitch off the tip of the left needle. You will now have one purl stitch on the right needle.

BINDING OFF

Using whichever stitch you are working in, knit (or purl) two stitches in the normal way. With the left needle, pick up the first stitch on the right needle (the one nearest you) (K) and bring it over the second stitch and let it slide off the needle. You will now be left with one loop on the right needle. Work another stitch onto the right needle and repeat the process. To finish off, cut the yarn and

K

draw the end through the final loop and pull tight.

Three-needle bind off

This method is used to join two pieces of knitting with an equal number of stitches to create a seamless join. You can see this method used in the Hooded top project on page 62.

Basic fabrics

All knitted fabrics are made by using either or both of the same two basic stitches – knit and purl.

GARTER STITCH (left)

This stitch is formed by knitting every row, producing the same pebbly pattern on the front and the back. It is loose and stretches equally in both directions. The same result is produced by purling every row.

STOCKINETTE STITCH (right)

This is the most common fabric stitch. It is formed by alternately knitting and purling rows. This creates a smooth fabric that is versatile and ideal for making garments, and is very stretchy horizontally. The side shown is the knitted side.

REVERSE STOCKINETTE STITCH (top left)

This is, as it sounds, the reverse side of stockinette stitch, the purled side, and is used to give a variation in texture.

SEED STITCH (bottom left)

This stitch forms a firmer fabric than the stockinette stitch and is created by alternately working 1 knit, 1 purl stitch. Stitches that are knitted on one row will be knitted on the next row and stitches that are purled on one row will be purled on the next row. For an odd number of stitches, the instructions will be as follows: K1, * p1, k1, rep from * to end. Repeat this row.

RIB STITCH (above)

This stitch creates a stretchy fabric, which is ideal for cuffs and edges. Work alternate knit and purl stitches. In subsequent rows, knit the knit stitches and purl the purl stitches. The most common are 1 x 1 (k1, p1) or 2 x 2 (k2, p2) ribbing, but any number of stitches can be used.

Shaping techniques

Garments are most commonly shaped by increasing or decreasing the number of stitches in a row. While the methods given here are the ones most suitable for patterns in this book, there are a number of different ways of increasing and decreasing the number of stitches, each of which creates a different appearance.

INCREASING

By increasing the number of stitches in a row the work becomes wider.

Yarn over (YO)

A stitch is formed by wrapping the yarn around the needle between two stitches. This method forms a hole in the fabric, and is used for decorative effect, or when making lacy fabric.

YO between two knit stitches

Bring the yarn forward, under the right needle, then over it to the back for the next knit stitch (A).

A

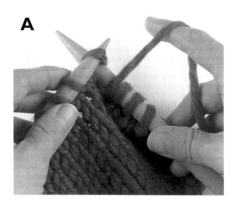

YO between two purl stitches

Take the yarn to the back, under the right needle, then over it to the front of the needle for the next purl stitch.

Raised increasing

A raised stitch is formed by picking up the horizontal strand between two stitches with the right needle and working it (in either knit or purl) like a stitch (B). Working into the front of the stitch gives a decorative hole. Working into the back twists the stitch so that the increase is almost invisible.

B

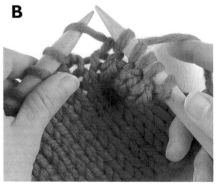

Working the same stitch twice

A stitch is made by working (in either knit or purl) first into the front, then into the back of a stitch (C).

C

DECREASING
By decreasing the number of stitches in a row, the fabric is made narrower.

Binding off
Binding stitches off at the beginning of a row is used when decreasing more than one stitch. It creates a step effect.

Working two stitches together
Working in knit stitch: insert the right needle from left to right into the second and first stitch on the left needle (D), knit two stitches together. Working in purl stitch: insert the right needle from right to left into the first and second stitch on the left needle, purl two stitches together.

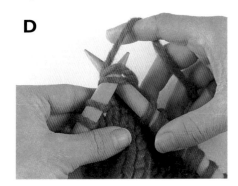

D

Slip stitch decreasing
Working in knit stitch: slip a stitch knitwise by inserting the needle from the left to the right of the stitch, as if to knit it. Knit the next stitch, insert the left needle into the front of the slipped stitch and pass it over the knitted one (E). Working in purl

E

stitch: slip a stitch purlwise by inserting the needle from the right to left of the stitch, as if to purl it. Purl the next stitch, insert the left needle into the front of the slipped stitch and pass it over the purled one.

Except when binding off stitches, decreasing pulls the stitches either to the left or to the right. In most cases this is not important except for when the stitches will be visible, such as at

the neck. In this case you want your stitches to slant to the left when working on the right side and to the right when working on the left side. To make the stitches slant to the right, knit or purl two stitches together (F).

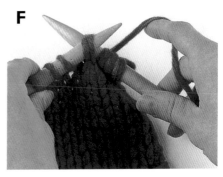

F

To make the stitches slant to the left you should knit or purl through the back loops only of the stitches (G).

G

Buttonholes

There are three basic ways of making a buttonhole: round eyelet, vertical and horizontal.

ROUND EYELET BUTTONHOLE (right)
This makes a small round hole that is used in baby clothes in particular. Bear in mind that with thicker yarns the hole will be larger. Make the hole so that it is in line with the button. With the right side facing, YO, k2tog.
Next row: Work all stitches, including the YO.

VERTICAL BUTTONHOLE (right)
Make the buttonhole so that the top finishes one row above the button – this will ensure the button doesn't pop out. Work each side separately

until the buttonhole has reached the depth that you require. Rejoin both parts, making sure that you have worked in the same direction for both sides.

HORIZONTAL BUTTONHOLE (left)

Make the buttonhole so that it finishes one stitch to the left of the button. Bind off the number of stitches required for the length of the buttonhole.

Next row: Work to one stitch before the beginning of the buttonhole, then increase by knitting into the front and back of the next stitch. Cast on the number of stitches you bound off on the previous row, less one.

TIP

When positioning buttons on a cardigan, bear in mind that the most important buttons are the ones at the neck, the bust and above the hem. Place these first and distribute the remaining buttons equally along the front opening.

Changing yarns and colors

The principles for attaching a new length of yarn and changing color are essentially the same.

ATTACHING NEW YARN

At the beginning of a row, tie the new yarn onto the old in a simple knot and slide the knot close to the needle. You can sew in the ends later. If the side edges of your project are going to be visible, it may be preferable to change a yarn mid-row and sew the ends in to the wrong side of the work.

WORKING IN HORIZONTAL STRIPES

For horizontal stripes, change colors at the end of the row, attaching the new color yarn to the old just as you would attach a new length of yarn (A). If you are repeating the color change every few rows you can carry the unused yarn up the side of the work; otherwise cut the yarn and rejoin later.

WORKING IN VERTICAL STRIPES

To make vertical stripes the yarn is changed mid-row, usually on the purl side. When you reach the point in the pattern that requires a new yarn color, tie the new yarn onto the old and move the knot up the yarn to the needle. In order to avoid a gap in the work, you need to twist the two yarns together. So when you make the next stitch in the new color, hold the new color to the right with your right hand and the old color to the left with your left hand (B). This way the two yarns will cross when you make the next stitch. This method is also used when creating motifs.

A

B

Finishing

Finishing is an essential part of making a garment. It is really worth spending some time on, even if it is tempting to rush the final stages. The success of a garment is the finish, so time and care are essential when pressing and joining pieces together.

BLOCKING AND PRESSING

This is the method of shaping the knitted pieces to specific dimensions using steam. First, weave all loose ends into a seam edge. Then lay the knitted piece on a padded board and pin into place. Measure the dimensions to ensure each piece is the correct size. You may need to slightly stretch or bunch the piece up. Now lay a damp cloth over the fabric and very gently press using a steam iron, paying special attention to the edges. These will be neater and easier to join if they have been pressed. Avoid pressing ribbing as this will flatten it.

SEAMS

To sew knitted pieces together, use a blunt-ended tapestry needle. Usually one or both of the shoulder seams are joined first so that you can work the neckband or collar.

There are two basic methods of joining seams: joining edge-to-edge and using a backstitch seam. Joining edge-to-edge creates an almost invisible seam. A backstitch seam is stronger, but creates a ridge. When working with thick yarns, the seams may be bulky. These can be pressed flat once the garment is complete.

Edge-to-edge seam — joining stockinette stitch edges

Joining two knitted edges with a mattress stitch creates an almost invisible seam.

Lay the two sections right side up and edge to edge, making sure the stitches are aligned. Attach the yarn at the right end and insert the needle under the horizontal bar next to the edge stitch of one section, then insert the needle under the corresponding bar of the other section. Continue by sewing into each stitch, zigzagging across from one section to the other until the end.

Edge-to-edge seam — joining bound-off edges

With the work right-side up, align the two sections. Attach the yarn at the right and, working right to left, bring the needle out in the center of the first stitch below the bound-off edge, insert the needle through the center of the first stitch on the opposite section and out through the center of the adjacent stitch.

Backstitch seam

Place the pieces to be joined together with their right sides facing inwards, ensuring that the stitches and rows are aligned. Sewing into the center of each stitch, bring the needle out one stitch in from the edge, insert the needle one stitch back and bring the needle out one stitch ahead of the emerging thread. Sew ¼ in. in from the edge of the knitting.

SLEEVES

As the top of the sleeve and the armhole into which it is set can be different shapes, care needs to be taken when inserting the sleeves so that the fabric doesn't pucker.

Once the shoulder seams have been joined, fold the sleeve in half lengthwise. Mark the center of the top of the sleeve and the midway points between the center and the underarm with pins.

On the main body of the garment, mark the center of the shoulder join and midway points from that point and the underarm with pins.

With right sides together, pin the sleeve into the armhole, matching up the marker pins. Using backstitch, sew the sleeve seam on the inside.

PICKING UP STITCHES

To finish off an edge or make a collar, you can pick up stitches around the edge and knit into them.

Where the pattern requires you to work more or less than one stitch into one loop, it is important to make sure that stitches are worked evenly along the edge; otherwise the fabric will pucker. Divide the work into equal sections and mark with pins, then calculate how many stitches will be needed for each section.

With the right side facing and the work in your left hand, insert the right needle into both loops of the first bound-off stitch, yarn over, and draw the loop through the stitch towards you. Work from right to left. When picking up stitches around a

curved neck edge, insert the needle into the center of the stitch below the shaping to avoid making an unsightly hole.

NECKBANDS

As you will be using straight needles throughout, you will be working in rows rather than rounds for the patterns in this book. Neckbands are made by joining the right shoulder and picking up and knitting into the stitches around the neck, working as many rows as instructed. You will then need to join up the other shoulder and the two sides of the neck.

Design your own sweater

The patterns in this book cover a wide spectrum of simple sweater shapes, and are easy to adapt, provided you make a few calculations before you start. Once you have made a few garments, you will have an idea of how they are composed and can think about designing a sweater from scratch.

PLANNING AND MEASURING

First decide on a basic shape and what type of sleeves and neckline your sweater will have. Next take accurate measurements for the bust, waist, hips, inside sleeve and armhole depth. Choose your yarn and the stitch you plan to use and work a swatch to check the gauge (see page 10).

Now you are ready to draw an outline. Include all the width and length measurements of each piece, making sure you have allowed enough for ease and 1/4 in. seams.

Begin by taking accurate measurements.

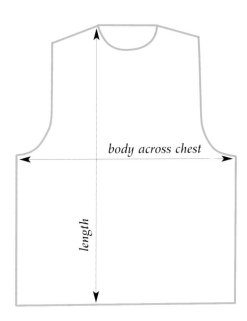

Most patterns measure the chest for length and body.

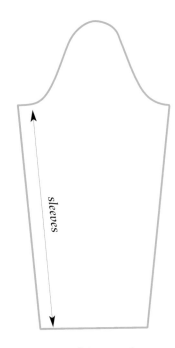

Sleeves are measured from underarm to wrist.

Calculate the number of stitches by multiplying the number of stitches per in. by the garment width. Calculate how many rows by multiplying the number of rows per in. by the garment length.

YARN REQUIREMENTS

Work out how much yarn you will need either by working on quantities used for a similar garment, or by weighing and measuring a swatch, then working out the rough surface area of your garment.

CHARTING YOUR GARMENT

Your garment will probably require some shaping for a good fit. For example, the bust should be wider than the waist, and the waist should be narrower than the hips. Calculate how many stitches you will require at the widest and narrowest points and how many rows are to be worked in between. Front and back shapings are usually the same, except at the neck.

Where possible, make shapings on the right side of the work, and be sure to increase or decrease evenly and gradually so that you don't have a "step" effect. When using bulky yarns simple shapes will work best.

Waist shaping

Subtract the number of stitches at the narrowest point (waist) from the number of stitches at the widest point (hips) and divide by two. This is the number of stitches you will need to decrease each side of the work to reach the width of the waist.

Bust shaping

Subtract the number of stitches at the narrowest point (waist) from the number of stitches at the widest point (bust) and divide by two. This is the number of stitches you will need to increase each side of the work to reach the width of the bust.

Armhole shaping

Except for a dolman (batwing) sleeve, you will need to bind off several stitches or the equivalent of 1-2 in. (2-5 cm) at the armhole for ease. Once you have decided which armhole shape you will be using (see Sleeves and armholes, page 20), calculate how many stitches you need to decrease to the top of the work or shoulder shaping.

Shoulder shaping

If you wish to gently shape the shoulders of your sweater, subtract the number of stitches you require for the neck from the number of stitches at the top of the armhole and divide by two. This gives you the number of stitches at each shoulder. To shape the shoulder, bind off a third to a half of the stitches in one row, and then the remaining stitches in the following row.

Neckline shaping

In most cases neckline shaping is only required at the front of the work and the back can be knitted straight across. As neckline shaping is very visible it needs to be worked with some care and attention. In most cases shaping should be worked on the right side, and each side of the neck worked separately.

As a rough guide for round necks, calculate that the neck should be about a third of the total width across the top. Half of those stitches are cast off in the middle and the remaining half are decreased evenly on each side.

Neckbands and collars

If you want to finish your sweater with a neckband, you can do so by picking up and knitting into stitches around the edge of the neck opening. Without double-pointed or circular needles you will not be able to knit in rounds, and will need to join the neckband when the desired length has been reached.

Sleeves and armholes

Sleeves are usually made by starting at the cuff and working upwards. As with body shaping, you will need to measure the narrowest point (wrist) and the widest point (underarm) to calculate how many stitches you will need to increase on each side of the sleeve. Increases should be worked gradually up the sleeve on the right side of the work.

There are several basic shapes for sleeves and armholes. The four most common shapes are: sleeveless, which requires little or no armhole shaping; the classic armhole with a set-in sleeve; the raglan armhole, which goes right up to the neck in a straight line; and the dolman armhole, which creates a batwing-type sleeve, where the sleeves are made as an extension of the width of the body. All four shapes are used in the patterns in this book.

Except for the drop-down shoulder, which requires no shaping, the armhole and top of a sleeve are shaped by decreasing stitches on either side of the work. First, bind off the same number of stitches as you bind off on the body at the underarm, then decrease symmetrically until the top of the sleeve shapings match the armhole.

ARMHOLE SHAPINGS

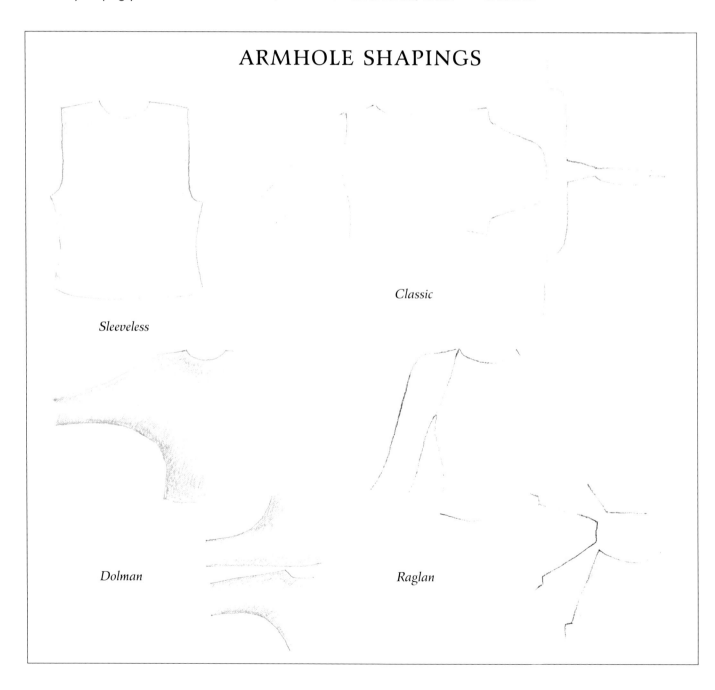

Sleeveless

Classic

Dolman

Raglan

Troubleshooting

If you are new to knitting it is all too easy to drop or pick up the odd knit stitch. Here are a few simple methods of correcting any errors you may make.

PICKING UP A DROPPED KNIT STITCH

Insert the right needle through the free loop (the stitch from the row below) and the strand (the stitch you need to recover). Insert the left needle through the loop only, from back to front (A), and pass the loop over the strand and off the needle.

The dropped stitch is now on the right needle, but facing the wrong way. Insert the left needle from front to back of the stitch and transfer across to left needle. You are now ready to knit into it.

A

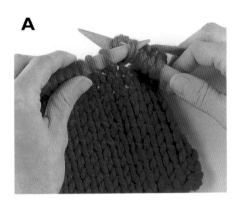

When recovering dropped stitches, take care not to twist the stitch, as this will ruin the appearance of your work (B).

B

PICKING UP A DROPPED PURL STITCH

Insert the right needle through the free loop (the stitch from the row below) and the strand. Now insert the left needle through the loop only, from front to back (C), and pass the loop over the strand and off the needle.

The dropped stitch is now on the right needle, but it is facing the wrong way. Insert the left needle from front to back of the stitch and transfer across to the left needle. You are now ready to purl into it.

C

RECOVERING A RUN IN STOCKINETTE STITCH

With the right side of the work facing, insert a crochet hook from front to back of the loop at the bottom of the run, hook it over the loose horizontal strand and draw through the loop (D). Continue as many times as necessary until you have repaired the run.

D

UNRAVELLING

If you have made an error several rows down, or if you are simply unhappy with the appearance of your work and want to knit it again, you will need to unravel the work in order to correct it. To do this, mark the row of the error with a bit of yarn or a marker. With the right side facing (yarn on the left), unravel to one row above the marker.

For knit stitches, hold the yarn at the back and insert the left needle from front to back of each stitch below. As you do so, pull out the stitch above (E). Continue until all of the stitches are on the left needle.

E

For purl stitches, hold the yarn at the front and insert the left needle from front to back of each stitch below. As you do so, pull out the stitch above. Continue until all of the stitches are on the left needle.

Skill rating:
Very easy

Rectangular wrap with tassels

This is a very simple pattern, easy enough for a beginner and made in one size. To give the fabric texture, stockinette stitch is interspersed with rows of reverse stockinette stitch. The wrap is finished off with tassels in a contrasting color at both ends.

Estimated time of project: 10 hours

Measurements
This pattern makes a reversible wrap that is 29½ x 59 in. (75 cm x 150 cm).

TIPS

When the ends of each row are exposed, such as with this wrap, it is important to ensure that your edges are straight and even. At the beginning of each row, pull the yarn snug to tighten up the last stitch of the previous row. You should also avoid joining new yarn at the end of the row as this will be visible.

Choose a contrast color for the tassels.

MATERIALS
7 balls of Rowan Big Wool in Pistachio
1 ball of Rowan Big Wool in Smoky
Pair of US 19 (15 mm) needles
US M (9 mm) crochet hook
8 in. (20 cm) square of cardboard

GAUGE
7½ stitches and 10 rows to 4 in. (10 cm) measured over stockinette stitch using US 19 (15 mm) needles.

WRAP
Cast on 56 sts using US 19 (15 mm) needles.
Rows 1–6: Starting with a knit row, work 6 rows in St st ending with a purl row.
Rows 7–10: Starting with a purl row, work 4 rows in reverse St st, ending with a knit row.
Repeat rows 1–10 until work is desired length.
Bind off.

TASSELS
Wrap both the Pistachio and Smoky wools around a 8 in. (20 cm) piece of cardboard 100 times. Cut the yarn along one edge and divide into bundles of five strands. This will give you ten tassels along each short edge. Fold each bundle in half and, starting at one edge of the wrap, draw the center of the bundle through a stitch with your crochet hook, making a loop. Now draw the ends through the loop and tighten. Place ten tassels evenly along each end of the wrap.

Big and easy poncho

This V-neck poncho is quick and straightforward to knit using super chunky yarn and easy shaping techniques. It is worked throughout in stockinette stitch in two pieces, the front and the back, which are then joined. This fabric is very stretchy, and thus the end result might be longer than the dimensions given here.

Estimated time of project: 5 hours

Measurements
To fit bust:

32	34	36	38	40	in.
81	86	91	97	102	cm

Actual measurements
Length:

29½	30¾	32	33	34¼	in.
75	78	81	84	87	cm

Width:

44¼	45¾	47	48½	50¼	in.
112.5	116	119.5	123	127.5	cm

The pattern gives the number of stitches for the smallest size first; larger sizes follow in brackets.

MATERIALS
10 (10:11:12:13) balls of Rowan Biggy Print in Allsorts
Pair of US 36 (20 mm) needles
Crochet hook
8 in. (20 cm) square of cardboard

GAUGE
5½ stitches and 7 rows to 4 in. (10 cm) measured over stockinette stitch using US 36 (20 mm) needles.

SPECIAL TERMS
Double decrease: Insert the needle from left to right into the second, then first stitch on the left needle and slip both stitches knitwise, knit 1 stitch, pass the two slipped stitches over the knitted one.
V-neck shaping: On the left side of the work knitting or purling two stitches together through the front two loops pulls the stitch to the right. On the right side of the work knitting or purling through the back two loops pulls the stitch to the left.

Double decreasing is used to shape the poncho.

TIPS

Always finish the row you are working on before leaving your knitting for the day and mark on the pattern which row you have completed. This will avoid confusion when you pick your work up again later.

BACK

Cast on 69 (71:73:75:77) sts using US 36 (20 mm) needles.
Beg with a knit row, work 2:2:2:2:4 rows in St st.
Next row: K33 (34:35:36:37), double decrease, k to end. Place a marker in the central stitch.
Next row: Purl.
Next row: Knit to within 1 st of the central marker, double decrease, knit to end.
Next row: Purl.
Repeat the last 2 rows 3 times more.
[59 (61:63:65:67) sts.]
Dec 1 st at each end of next and every foll 4th row **and at the same time** double decrease at the center of the work on next and every foll alt row until 49 (45:45:47:51) sts rem, ending with a WS row.
Dec 1 st at each end of next and every following alt row **and at the same time** double decrease at the center of the work on next and every foll alt row until 9 (9:9:11:11) sts rem, ending with a WS row.
Bind off.

FRONT

Work as for back until 25 (25:25:27:27) sts rem, ending with a WS row.

Left side of neck

Work both sides of neck separately:
Next row: K2tog, k8 (8:8:9:9), k2tog and turn, leaving rem sts on a holder.
Next row: P2tog, purl to end.
Next row: K2tog, knit to last 2 sts, k2tog.
Next row: P2tog, purl to end.
Repeat the last 2 rows once more. [3:3:3:4:4 sts.]
Next row: K2tog, k1 (1:1:0:0), K2tog 0 (0:0:1:1) time.
Next row: P2tog.
Fasten off rem st.

Right side of neck

With RS facing, rejoin yarn at center of work, bind off 1 st, k2tog tbl, k8 (8:8:9:9), k2tog.

Next row: Purl to last 2 sts, p2tog tbl.
Next row: K2tog tbl, knit to last 2 sts, k2tog.
Rep the last 2 rows once more. [4(4:4:5:5) sts.]
Next row: Purl to last two sts, p2tog tbl.
Next row: (K2tog tbl) 0 (0:0:1:1) time, K1(1:1:0:0), K2tog.
Next row: P2tog tbl.
Fasten off rem sts.

FINISHING

Press both pieces carefully. Join side seams.

Tassels (optional)

To make tassels follow the instructions on page 22, bearing in mind that this yarn is very thick, so you may want to use fewer strands. Place twenty 6 in. (15 cm) tassels evenly along each of the four side edges of the poncho.

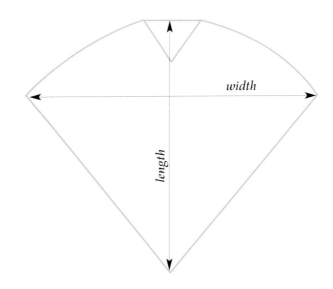

Basic shape for a poncho.

Mohair shawl

Skill rating:
Very easy

This fluffy mohair shawl is quick and very easy to make, with no sewing or pressing required. It is made by knitting a large triangle in garter stitch, simply increasing one stitch in each row. Using a fine yarn on large needles creates an open and lacy look, but a fluffy mohair will still be very warm. The garter stitch makes the garment very stretchy.

Estimated time of project: 10 hours

Measurements
This pattern makes a shawl 41¼ x 90½ in. (105 cm x 230 cm).

TIPS
Check your work often for any mistakes or dropped stitches, which can be hard to detect in a fluffy wool. Also be aware that a fluffy yarn is more difficult to unravel than a smooth one, so if possible, try to catch mistakes as they happen.

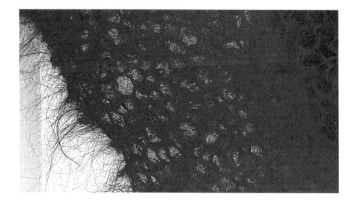

MATERIALS
4 balls of Texere Destiny Mohair in Fuchsia
Pair of US 15 (10 mm) needles

GAUGE
8 stitches and 10 rows to 4 in. (10 cm) measured over garter stitch using US 15 (10 mm) needles.
As this is not a fitted garment, the gauge is not very important. By using large needles you'll create a light, open look, but you can use smaller needles if you wish to make a denser fabric. The proportions of the shawl will be the same.

SHAWL
Cast on 3 sts using US 15 (10 mm) needles.
Working in g st, knit each row increasing 1 st in the 2nd st of every row as follows:
Knit 1 st, knit into the front and back of the 2nd st (making 1 new st), knit to end.
Cont until work measures 41¼ in. (105 cm) in length. At this point, with the stitches still on the needle, it may appear that the shawl will be long and narrow and not wide enough at the top, however there will be ample stitches to make the shawl very wide. The final important stage is to bind off **very** loosely. This will give you as much widthwise stretch as you need.

Mohair creates a wonderful, lacy texture.

Skill rating:
Easy

Batwing sleeve sweater

Knitting a sweater doesn't get much simpler than this. The batwing or dolman sleeve is made by adding stitches onto the body as you work upwards, so the sweater is created in just two pieces, which are then sewn together. The effect is a relaxed look, with a sleeve that is wide under the arm. This works especially well in a soft yarn like chenille.

Estimated time of project: 10 hours

Measurements
To fit bust:

32	34	36	38	40	in.
81	86	91	97	102	cm

Actual measurements
Total width (measured from wrist to wrist):

60	60¼	64	65¼	66½	in.
154	157	164	167	170	cm

Length:

20½	21	21	22	22	in.
52	53	53	56	56	cm

The pattern gives the number of stitches for the smallest size first; larger sizes follow in brackets.

MATERIALS
6 (6:6:7:7) balls of Sirdar Wow in Imperial Purple
Pair of US 15 (10 mm) needles
Chenille needle or a length of smooth yarn in a matching color to sew the seams

GAUGE
6 stitches and 10 rows to 4 in. (10 cm) measured over stockinette stitch using US 15 (10 mm) needles.

BACK
Cast on 30 (32:34:36:38) sts using US 15 (10 mm) needles.
Beg with a knit row, work in st st until work measures 8½ (9:9:9½:9½) in. (22 (23:23:24:24) cm), ending with a WS row.

Underarm shaping
Increase 2 sts at each end of the next 2 rows.
[38 (40:42:44:46) sts.]

Arm shaping – lower edge
Cast on 3 (3:4:4:4) sts at beg of next 2 rows. (Note: you will need to cast on purlwise at beg of purl row).
[44 (46:48:52:54) sts.]
Cast on 8 sts at beg of next 6 rows.

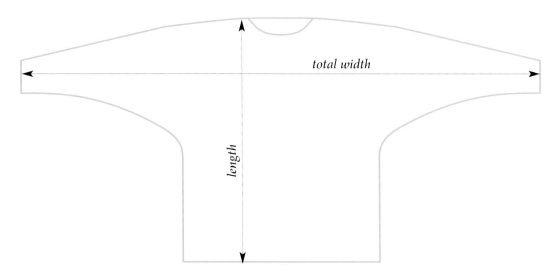

Because of the sleeve shape, the width is measured from wrist to wrist.

[92 (94:98:100:102) sts.]
Work 10 (10:10:12:12) rows without shaping, ending with a WS row.

Arm shaping – upper edge
Bind off 8 sts at beg of next 4 rows, then 7 sts at beg of foll 4 rows. [32 (34:38:40:42) sts.]

Shoulder shaping
Bind off 4 sts at beg of next 2 rows.
Bind off 4 (5:6:7:7) sts at beg of foll 2 rows.
Transfer rem 16 (16:18:18:20) sts to a holder.

FRONT
Work as for back until arm shaping – upper edge.
Bind off 8 sts at beg of next 4 rows.
[60 (62:66:68:70) sts.]

Shape neck
Work each side of neck separately.
Next row: Bind off 7 sts, knit until there are 18 (19:20:21:21) sts on right needle and turn, leaving rem sts on a holder.
Next row: P2tog, purl to end.
Next row: Bind off 7 sts, knit to last 2 sts, k2tog.
Next row: P2tog, purl to end. [8 (9:10:11:12) sts.]

Shoulder shaping
Bind off 4 sts at beg of next row.
Work 1 row.
Bind off rem 4 (5:6:7:7) sts.

Transfer center 10 (10:12:14:14) sts to a holder and with RS facing, rejoin yarn to rem sts, knit to end.
Next row: Bind off 7 sts, purl to last 2 sts, p2tog.
Next row: K2tog, knit to end.
Next row: Bind off 7 sts, purl to last 2 sts, p2tog. [8 (9:10:11:11) sts.]
Work 1 row, ending with a RS row.

Shoulder shaping
Bind off 4 sts at beg of next row.
Work 1 row.
Bind off rem 4 (5:6:7:7) sts.

FINISHING
When sewing seams you should use either a chenille needle, which is sharper and has a larger eye than a tapestry needle, or a smooth yarn of the same color, because chenille has a tendency to disintegrate when used in sewing. Sew up the top of the right sleeve, leaving the left shoulder open.

Neckband
With RS facing, pick up and knit 7 sts down right side of neck, knit 10 (10:12:14:14) sts across front, pick up and knit 7 sts up left side and knit 16 (16:18:18:20) sts across back. [40 (40:44:44:48) sts.]
Beg with a purl row, work 2 rows in St st.
Bind off purlwise.

Join the neckband. Sew up the top of the left sleeve. Sew up both side and lower sleeve seams.

Cropped turtleneck

This short and slim-fitting turtleneck is a straightforward and speedy project, using the chunkiest yarn and giant US 36 (20 mm) needles. It is worked throughout in stockinette stitch and finished with a roll-down turtleneck.

Estimated time of project: 7½ hours

Measurements
To fit bust:

31½	34	36	38	40	in.
80	86	91	97	102	cm

Actual measurements
Body across chest:

15¾	17	18¾	20	21½	in.
40	43.5	47.5	51	54.5	cm

Length:

19	19¼	19¾	20	20½	in.
48	49	50	51	52	cm

Sleeves (measured from underarm to wrist):

17	17	17¼	17¼	17¼	in.
43	43	44	44	44	cm

The pattern gives the number of stitches for the smallest size first; larger sizes follow in brackets.

MATERIALS
8 (8:9:9:10) balls of Rowan Biggy Print in Splash
Pair of US 36 (20 mm) needles

GAUGE
5½ stitches and 7 rows to 4 in. (10 cm) measured over stockinette stitch using US 36 (20 mm) needles.

BACK
Cast on 22 (24:26:28:30) sts using US 36 (20 mm) needles.
Beg with a knit row, work in st st until work measures 11¾ (12¼:12¼:12½:12½) in. (30 (31:31:32:32) cm), ending with a WS row.

Shape armholes
Bind off 3 sts at beg of next 2 rows.
[16 (18:20:22:24) sts.]
Dec 1 st at each end of the next 0 (0:0:0:1) row.
[16 (18:20:22:22) sts.]
Cont without shaping until the armhole measures 7 (7:7½:7½:8) in. (18 (18:19:19:20) cm), ending with a WS row.

Shape shoulders
Bind off 2 (2:3:3:3) sts at beg of the next 2 rows.
Bind off 2 (3:3:4:4) sts at beg of next 2 rows.
Transfer rem 8 sts to a holder.

FRONT

Work as for back until 2 rows less have been worked to beg of shoulder shaping, ending with a WS row.

Shape neck and shoulder

Work each side of neck separately.
Next row: Knit 6 (7:8:8:8) sts and turn, leaving rem sts on a holder.
Dec 1 st at neck edge of next row. [5 (6:7:7:7) sts.]
Bind off 2 (2:2:3:3) sts at beg of row, dec 1 (1:1:0:0) st at neck edge. [2 (3:4:4:4) sts.]
Work 1 row.
Bind off rem 2 (3:4:4:4) sts.
Transfer center 4 (4:4:6:6) sts to a holder.
With RS facing, rejoin yarn to rem sts, knit to end.
[6 (7:8:8:8) sts.]
Dec 1 st at neck edge of next row. [5 (6:7:7:7) sts.]
Dec 1 (1:1:0:0) st at neck edge of next row.
[4 (5:6:7:7) sts.]
Bind off 2 (2:2:3:3) sts at beg of next row.
Work 1 row.
Bind off rem 2 (3:4:4:4) sts.

SLEEVES (make 2)

Cast on 13 (13:15:15:17) sts using US 36 (20 mm) needles.
Beg with a knit row, work in St st and shape sides by inc 1 st at each end of 9th and every foll 6th row until there are 19 (19:21:21:23) sts.
Cont without shaping until sleeve measures 17 (17:17¼:17¼:17¼) in. (43 (43:44:44:44) cm), ending with a WS row.

Shape top of sleeve

Bind off 3 sts at beg of next 2 rows.
[13 (13:15:15:17) sts.]
Dec 1 st at each end of next and foll 3 (3:4:4:4) alt rows. [5 (5:5:5:7) sts.]
Work 1 (1:2:2:2) rows.
Bind off rem 5 (5:5:5:7) sts.

FINISHING

Press all pieces carefully. Join right shoulder seam.

Turtleneck

With RS facing, pick up and knit 6 sts down left side of neck, knit 4 (4:4:6:6) sts from front, pick up and knit 6 sts up right side of neck, knit 8 sts from back.
[24 (24:24:26:26) sts.]
Beg with a knit row, work in st st until collar measures 8½ in. (22 cm), ending with a purl row. When the neck is folded down, the knit side will be on the right side. Bind off very loosely.
Join left shoulder seam and turtleneck. Join side seams. Join sleeve seams. Set sleeves into the armholes.

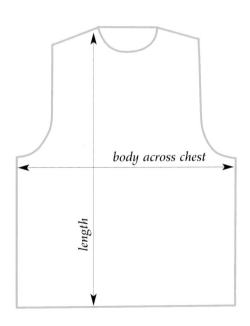

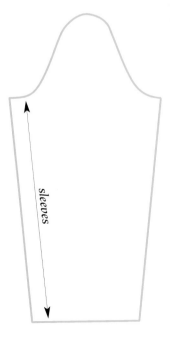

Basic shapes for a cropped turtleneck.

Loose-fit turtleneck

This big winter sweater can be knitted up in no time using the thickest wool on giant needles. The end result is a sweater is that is loose and free with a roll-down neck. If the pattern seems to be coming up smaller than you had expected, don't worry as the yarn has plenty of give and will stretch.

Estimated time of project: 10 hours

Measurements
To fit bust:

32	34	36	38	40	in.
81	86	91	97	102	cm

Actual measurements
Body across chest:

20¾	22¼	23½	25	26½	in.
53	56.5	60	63.5	67.5	cm

Length:

25½	26	26½	26¾	27½	in.
65	66	67	68	70	cm

Sleeves (measured from underarm to wrist):

18	18	18	19	19	in.
46	46	46	48	48	cm

The pattern gives the number of stitches for the smallest size first; larger sizes follow in brackets.

MATERIALS
12 (13:14:15:16) balls of Rowan Biggy Print in Razzle Dazzle
Pair of US 36 (20 mm) needles

GAUGE
5½ stitches and 7 rows to 4 in. (10 cm) measured over stockinette stitch using US 36 (20 mm) needles.

BACK
Cast on 29 (31:33:35:37) sts using US 36 (20 mm) needles.
Beg with a knit row, work in St st until work measures 16½ (17:17:17¼:17¾) in. (42 (43:43:44:45) cm), ending with a WS row.

Shape armholes
Bind off 3 sts at beg of next 2 rows.
[23 (25:27:29:31) sts.]
Cont without shaping until armhole measures 9 (9:9½:9½:10) in. (23 (23:24:24:25) cm), ending with a WS row.

Shape back, neck and shoulders
Work each side of neck separately.
Next row: Bind off 3 (3:3:4:4) sts, knit until there are 5 (6:6:6:6) sts on right needle and turn, leaving rem sts on a holder.
Next row: Dec 1 st at beg of row, purl to end.

The neck of the sweater can be easily rolled over.

Bind off remaining 4 (5:5:5:5) sts.
Transfer center 7 (7:9:9:11) sts to a holder.
With RS facing, rejoin yarn to rem sts, knit to end.
[8 (9:9:10:10) sts.]
Next row: Bind off 3 (3:3:4:4) sts, purl to last 2 sts, p2tog.
Work 1 row.
Bind off rem 4 (5:5:5:5) sts.

FRONT
Work as for back until 2 rows less have been worked to beg of back neck and shoulder shaping, ending with

a WS row.
Shape neck and shoulder
Work each side of neck separately.
Next row: Knit 7 (8:8:9:9) sts, k2tog and turn, leaving rem sts on a holder.
Next row: Dec 1 st at beg of row, purl to end.
Next row: Bind off 3 (3:3:4:4) sts, knit to end.
Work 1 row.
Bind off rem 4 (5:5:5:5) sts.
Transfer center 5 (5:7:7:9) sts to a holder.
With RS facing, rejoin yarn to rem sts, k2tog, knit to end. [8 (9:9:10:10) sts.]
Next row: Purl to last 2 sts, p2tog.
Work 1 row.
Bind off 3 (3:3:4:4) sts at beg of next row.
Work 1 row.
Bind off rem 4 (5:5:5:5) sts.

SLEEVES (make 2)
Cast on 17 (19:19:21:21) sts using US 36 (20 mm) needles.
Beg with a knit row, work in St st and shape sides by inc 1 st at each end of 5th and every foll 6th row until there are 23 (23:25:25:27) sts.

Cont without shaping until sleeve measures 46 (46:46:48:48) cm (18 (18:18:19:19) in), ending with a WS row.
Bind off loosely.

FINISHING
Press all pieces carefully. Join right shoulder seam.

Collar
With RS facing, pick up and knit 5 sts down left side of front neck, knit 5 (5:7:7:9) sts from front, pick up and knit 5 sts up right side of front neck and 4 sts down right side of back neck, knit 7 (7:9:9:11) sts from back, pick up and knit 4 sts up left side of back neck. [30 (30:34:34:38) sts.]
Beg with a knit row, work in stockinette stitch until collar measures 10 in. (25 cm), ending with a purl row. When the collar is folded down, the knit side will be on the right side.
Bind off very loosely.

Join left shoulder seam. Sew up collar with a flat, invisible seam. Ease sleeves into armholes and sew into place. Join side and sleeve seams.

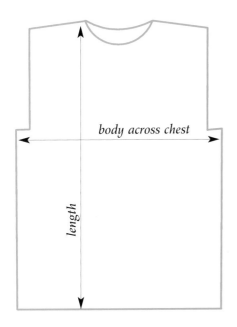
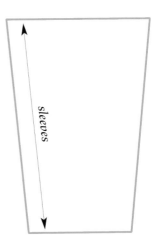

Basic shapes for a loose-fit turtleneck.

Skill rating:
Medium

V-neck sweater

This is a close fitting, but not tight sweater, worked throughout in stockinette stitch. It is slightly shaped in the body to give a fitted look, with a deep V at the neckline. With its variable thickness and colors, the yarn gives an interesting and non-uniform appearance.

Estimated time of project: 7 hours

Measurements
To fit bust:

32	34	36	38	40	in.
81	86	91	97	102	cm

Actual measurements
Body across chest:

16¾	17¾	19	20	21	in.
42.5	45.5	48	50.5	53	cm

Length:

19¼	19¼	20½	20½	21¾	in.
49	49	52	52	55	cm

Sleeves (measured from underarm to wrist):

17½	17½	17½	18	18	in.
44	44	44	46	46	cm

The pattern gives the number of stitches for the smallest size first; larger sizes follow in brackets.

MATERIALS
6 (6:6:7:7) balls of Colinette Point Five in Neptune
Pair of US 19 (15 mm) needles

GAUGE
7½ stitches and 10 rows to 4 in. (10 cm) measured over stockinette stitch using US 19 (15 mm) needles.

SPECIAL TERMS
V-neck shaping: on the left side of the work, knitting or purling two stitches together through the front two loops pulls the stitch to the right. On the right side of the work, knitting or purling through the back two loops pulls the stitch to the left.

BACK
Cast on 28 (30:32:34:36) sts using US 19 (15 mm) needles.
Beg with a knit row, work in St st.
Shape side seams by inc 1 st at each end of 15th (15th:17th:17th:19th) and foll 4th row.
[32 (34:36:38:40) sts.]
Cont without shaping until work measures 11 (11:11¾:11¾:12½) in. (28 (28:30:30:32) cm), ending with a WS row.

Shape armholes
Bind off 2 sts at beg of next 2 rows.
[28 (30:32:34:36) sts.]
Dec 1 st at each end of next row and foll 2 alt rows.
[22 (24:26:28:30) sts.]

Cont without shaping until armhole measures 6½ (6½:7:7:7½) in. (17 (17:18: 18:19) cm), ending with a WS row.

Shape back neck
Work each side of neck separately.
Next row: K7 (8:9:9:10) sts and turn, leaving rem sts on a holder.
Next row: P2tog, purl to end.
Work 2 rows.
Bind off rem 6 (7:8:8:9) sts.
With RS facing, rejoin yarn to rem sts, cast off center 8 (8:8:10:10) sts, knit to end.
Next row: Purl 5 (6:7:7:8) sts, p2tog.
Work 2 rows.
Bind off rem 6 (7:8:8:9) sts.

FRONT
Work as for back until front matches back to beg of armhole shaping, ending with a WS row.

Shape armholes
Bind off 2 sts at beg of next 2 rows.
[28 (30:32:34:36) sts.]

Shape left side of neck and armhole
Work each side of neck separately.
Next row: K2tog, k12 (13:14:15:16) sts and turn, leaving rem sts on a holder.
Next row: P2tog, purl to end.
Next row: K2tog, knit to end.
Next row: P2tog, purl to end.
Repeat the last 2 rows once more. [8 (9:10:11:12) sts.]
Cont to dec 1 st at neck edge on every foll alt row until 6 (7:8:8:9) sts remain. Cont without shaping until front matches back to bind-off, ending with a WS row. Bind off.

Shape right side of neck and armhole
With RS facing, rejoin yarn at the center, knit to last 2 sts, k2tog at armhole edge. [13 (14:15:16:17) sts.]
Next row: Purl to last 2 sts, p2tog tbl.
Next row: Knit to last 2 sts, k2tog.
Repeat the last 2 rows once more.
[9 (10:11:12:13) sts.]
Cont to dec 1 st at neck edge on next and every foll alt row until 6 (7:8:8:9) sts rem. Cont without shaping until front matches back to bind-off, ending with a WS row. Bind off.

SLEEVES (make 2)

Cast on 19 (19:19:21:21) sts using US 19 (15 mm) needles.

Beg with a knit row, work in St st and shape sides by inc 1 st at each end of 9th and every foll 10th (10th:8th:10th:8th) row until there are 27 (27:29:29:31) sts.

Work 5 (5:3:7:5) more rows, ending with a WS row.

Shape top of sleeve

Bind off 2 sts at beg of next 2 rows.
[23 (23:25:25:27) sts.]
Dec 1 st at each end of next and foll 2 alt rows.
[17 (17:19:19:21) sts.]
Work 3 (3:3:5:5) rows, ending with a WS row.
Bind off.

FINISHING

Press all pieces carefully. As this wool is not of uniform thickness, extra care should be taken with the seams to ensure that they are even and that there are no gaps. Join shoulder seams. Join side seams. Join sleeve seams. Insert the sleeves. To do this, gently manipulate the sleeve tops into the armholes so that the sleeve is evenly distributed and doesn't bunch; it may help to pin the sleeves in place first.

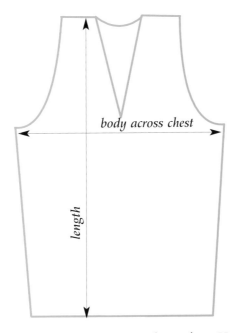
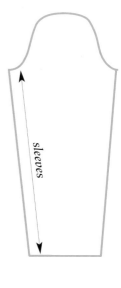

Basic shapes for a V-neck sweater.

Left: Take extra care when joining seams because this yarn is not of uniform thickness.

Raglan sleeve sweater

This sweater is worked mainly in stockinette stitch, with seed stitch decoration at the cuffs, edges and neck. The raglan sleeve means that the tops of the sleeves are sharply shaped and continue right up to the neck edge, giving the garment a clean and well-defined look.

Estimated time of project: 9 hours

Measurements
To fit bust:

32	34	36	38	40	in.
81	86	91	97	102	cm

Actual measurements
Body across chest:

17¼	18¼	19½	20½	21½	in.
44	46.5	49.5	52	54.5	cm

Length:

18¾	18¾	20½	20½	22	in.
48	48	52	52	56	cm

Sleeves (measured from underarm to wrist):

17¾	17¾	17¾	18½	18½	in.
45	45	45	47	47	cm

The pattern gives the number of stitches for the smallest size; larger sizes follow in brackets.

MATERIALS
5 (5:6:7:8) balls of Rowan Big Wool in Whoosh
Pair of US 19 (15 mm) needles
Pair of US 17 (12 mm) needles

GAUGE
7½ stitches and 10 rows to 4 in. (10 cm) measured over stockinette stitch using US 19 (15 mm) needles.

BACK
Cast on 29 (31:33:35:37) sts using US 17 (12 mm) needles.
Work 6 rows in seed stitch to create a decorative and fitted edge as follows:
Row 1: *k1, p1*, repeat pattern from * to last st, k1.
Repeat this row five times more.

Change to US 19 (15 mm) needles and, beg with a knit row, work in St st.
Shape side seams by inc 1 st at each end of 7th and foll 4th row. [33 (35:37:39:41) sts.]
Continue without shaping until work measures 11 (11:11¾:11¾:12½) in. (28 (28:30:30:32) cm), ending with a WS row.

*The edges, neck and cuffs are finished with
an attractive seed stitch border.*

Shape raglan armholes

Bind off 2 sts at beg of next 2 rows.
[29 (31:33:35:37) sts.]
Dec 1 st at each end of next row and every alt row
until 11 (13:13:15:15) sts rem.
Work 1 row, ending with a WS row.
Transfer rem sts to a holder.

FRONT

Work as for back until 17 (19:19:21:21) sts rem,
ending with a WS row.

Shape neck and raglan armhole

Work each side of neck separately.
Next row: K2tog, k4 sts and turn, leaving rem sts on a
holder.
Next row: P2tog, p3.
Next row: K2tog, k2.

Next row: Purl.
Next row: K2tog, k1.
Next row: P2tog. Cut yarn and pull through remaining loop.
Transfer center 5 (7:7:9:9) sts to a holder. With RS facing, rejoin yarn to rem sts, knit to last 2 sts, k2tog. [5 sts.]
Next row: P3, p2tog.
Next row: K2, k2tog.
Next row: Purl.
Next row: K1, k2tog.
Next row: P2tog. Cut yarn and pull through remaining loop.

SLEEVES (make 2)

Cast on 19 (19:19:21:21) sts using US 17 (12 mm) needles.
Work 6 rows in seed stitch to create a decorative cuff as follows:
Row 1: *k1, p1*, rep patt from * to last st, k1.
Repeat this row 5 times more.
Change to US 19 (15 mm) needles and, beg with a knit row, work in St st. Shape sides by inc 1 st at each end of 5th and every foll 10th (10th:8th:10th:8th) row until there are 27 (27:29:29:31) sts.
Cont to work without shaping until sleeve measures 17¾ (17¾: 17¾:18½:18½) in. (45 (45: 45:47:47) cm), ending with a WS row.

Sleeve shaping

Bind off 2 sts at beg of next 2 rows.
[23 (23:25:25:27) sts.]
Dec 1 st at each end of next and every foll alt row until 5 sts remain.
Work 1 row, ending with a WS row.
Bind off rem sts.

FINISHING

Press all pieces carefully. Using backstitch, join the sleeves to the body along the two front raglan seams and the right back seam. Leave the left back seam unstitched for now.

Collar

With RS facing and US 17 (12 mm) needles, pick up and knit 3 sts from the left sleeve and 6 sts down left side of neck, k5 (7:7:9:9) sts across front, pick up and knit 7 sts up right side of neck and 3 sts from the right sleeve, then knit 11 (13:13:15:15) sts across back.
[35 (39:39:43:43) sts.]
Work 6 rows in seed stitch as follows:
Row 1: *k1, p1*, rep patt from * to last st, k1.
Repeat this row 5 times more.
Bind off very loosely in seed stitch.

Join collar seam. Join left back raglan seam. Join side and sleeve seams.

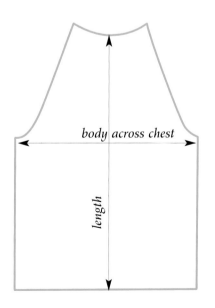

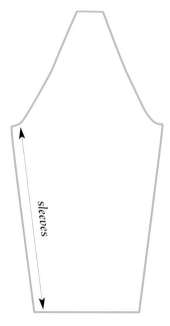

Basic shapes for a raglan sleeve sweater.

Skill rating:
Easy

Mohair T-shirt

Although mohair is not a thick yarn, it is very warm and fluffy and, when worked on large needles, it creates an open lacy texture. This T-shirt is finished off with ribbing and tied with a ribbon at the neck.

Estimated time of project: 6½ hours

Measurements
To fit bust:

32	34	36	38	40	in.
81	86	91	97	102	cm

Actual measurements
Body across chest:

10	10¾	11½	12¼	12¾	in.
25.5	27.5	29	31	32.5	cm

Length:

18½	19¼	20	21	21½	in.
47	49	51	53	55	cm

The pattern gives the number of stitches for the smallest size first; larger sizes follow in brackets.

MATERIALS
2 (2:2:3:3) balls of Texere Destiny Mohair in Muted Jade
3 ft (1 m) of ribbon
Pair of US 15 (10 mm) needles
Pair of US 17 (12 mm) needles

GAUGE
8 stitches and 10 rows to 4 in. (10 cm) measured over stockinette stitch using US 17 (12 mm) needles.

BACK
Cast on 30 (32:34:36:38) sts using US 15 (10 mm) needles.
Work in 2 x 2 rib:
Row 1: *k2, p2* rep patt from * to last 2 (0:2:0:2) sts, k2 (0:2:0:2).
Row 2: P2 (0:2:0:2), *k2, p2* rep patt to end.
Repeat rows 1 and 2 twice more.
Change to US 17 needles (12 mm). Beg with a knit row, work in St st.

Shape waist

Dec 1 st at beg of 5th (5th:5th:7th:7th) row.
[28 (30:32:34:36) sts.]
Cont to work in st st without shaping until back
measures 11½ (11¾:12¼:12½:13) in.
(29 (30:31:32:33) cm), ending with a WS row.

Shape armholes

Bind off 2 sts at beg of next 2 rows.
[24 (26:28:30:32) sts.]
Dec 1 st at each end of next and foll alt row.
[20 (22:24:26:28) sts.]
Cont without shaping until armhole measures
18 (19:20:21:22) cm (7 (7½:8:8¼:8¾) in), ending with
a WS row.

Shape shoulders

Bind off 3 sts at beg of next 2 rows.
Bind off 3 (3:4:4:4) sts at beg of next 2 rows.
Transfer rem 8 (10:10:12:14) sts to a holder.

FRONT
Work as for back until 2 rows less have been worked
to beg of shoulder shaping, ending with a WS row.

Shape neck and shoulder

Work each side of neck separately.
Next row: K9 (9:10:10:10) sts and turn, leaving rem
sts on a holder.
Next row: Bind off 2 sts purlwise, purl to end.
[7 (7:8:8:8) sts.]
Next row: Bind off 3 sts, k to last 2 sts, k2tog.
[3 (3:4:4:4) sts.]
Work 1 row.
Bind off rem 3 (3:4:4:4) sts.
Transfer center 2 (4:4:6:8) sts to a holder.
With RS facing, rejoin yarn to rem sts, k to end.
[9 (9:10:10:10) sts.]
Work 1 row.
Next row: Bind off 2 sts k to end.
Next row: Bind off 3 sts, p to last 2 sts, p2tog.
[3 (3:4:4:4) sts.]
Work 1 row.
Bind off rem 3 (3:4:4:4) sts.

SLEEVES (make 2)

Cast on 20 (22:22:24:26) sts using US 15 (10 mm) needles.

Work in 2 x 2 rib:

Row 1: *K2, p2* rep patt to last 0 (2:2:0:2) sts, k0 (2:2:0:2).

Row 2: P 0 (2:2:0:2), *k2, p2*, rep patt to end.

Rep rows 1 and 2 twice more.

Change to US 17 (12 mm) needles. Beg with a knit row, work in St st.

Inc 1 st at each end of next and foll alt row.

[24 (26:26:28:30) sts.]

Work 3 (3:3:5:5) rows, ending with a WS row.

Shape top of sleeve

Bind off 2 sts at beg of next 2 rows.

[20 (22:22:24:26) sts.]

Dec 1 st at each end of next and foll alt row.

[16 (18:18:20:22) sts.]

Work 3 rows.

Dec 1 st at each end of next and every foll alt row until 8 sts rem, ending with a WS row.

Bind off.

FINISHING

Join right shoulder seam.

Neckband

With RS facing, using US 15 (10 mm) needles, pick up and knit 7 sts down left side of neck, k2 (4:4:6:8) sts from front, pick up and knit 7 sts up right side of neck, k8 (10:10:12:14) sts from back.

[24 (28:28:32:36) sts.]

Work in 2 x 2 rib:

Row 1: *k2, p2*, rep patt from * to end.

Rep row 1 three times more.

Bind off.

Pin left shoulder and insert sleeves into armholes. Join side and sleeve seams. To finish off, lace a ribbon in each st on each side of the left shoulder and neck.

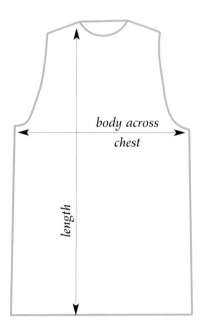

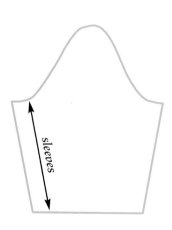

Basic shapes for a mohair T-shirt

Round-neck tank top

Knitted in lightweight cotton denim yarn, this tank top is perfect for summertime. Although gently shaped at the waist, it is still loose and flexible. It is worked in stockinette stitch.

Estimated time of project: 5 hours

Measurements
To fit bust:

32	34	36	38	40	in.
81	86	91	97	102	cm

Actual measurements
Body across chest:

14½	15¾	16½	17½	18¾	in.
37	40	42.5	45	48	cm

Length:

19	19½	20	20¾	21¼	in.
48	49.5	51	52.5	54	cm

The pattern gives the number of stitches for the smallest size; larger sizes follow in brackets.

MATERIALS
2 (3:3:3:3) balls of Sirdar Ultra Denim in Starling
Pair of US 17 (12 mm) needles

GAUGE
7½ stitches and 10 rows to 4 in. (10 cm) measured over stockinette stitch using US 17 (12 mm) needles.

BACK
Cast on 28 (30:32:34:36) sts using US 17 (12 mm) needles.
Beg with a knit row, work in St st.

Shape waist
Dec 1 st at each end of 5th and foll 4th row.
[24 (26:28:30:32) sts.]
Work 5 (5:5:7:7) rows, ending with a WS row.
Inc 1 st at each end of next row and foll 4th row.
[28 (30:32:34:36) sts.]
Cont until work measures 11½ (11¾:11¾:12:12) in. (29 (30:30:31:31) cm), ending with a WS row.

Shape armholes
Bind off 2 sts at beg of next 2 rows.
[24 (26:28:30:32) sts.]
Dec 1 st at each end of next and foll alt row.
[20 (22:24:26:28) sts.]
Cont without shaping until armhole measures 6¾ (6¾:7:7:7¼) in. (17 (17:18:18:19) cm), ending with a WS row.

The lightweight cotton denim yarn lets the wearer stay cool in summertime.

TIPS

Take care when picking up stitches around the neck to create a neck band. Where there is shaping, insert the needle into the center of the stitch in the row below the edge for a neater look.

Shape back neck

Work each side of neck separately.

Next row: K6 (7:7:8:9) sts and turn, leaving rem sts on a stitch holder.

Next row: (P2tog) twice, purl to end.

Bind off rem 4 (5:5:6:7) sts.

Transfer center 8 (8:10:10:10) sts to a holder. With RS facing, rejoin yarn to rem sts, knit to end. [6 (7:7:8:9) sts.]

Next row: Purl to last 4 sts, (p2tog) twice.

Bind off rem 4 (5:5:6:7) sts.

FRONT

Work as for back until 4 rows less have been worked to beg of neck shaping, ending with a WS row.

Shape neck

Work each side of neck separately.

Next row: K7 (8:8:9:10) sts and turn, leaving rem sts on a holder.

Next row: P2tog, purl to end.

Next row: Knit to last 2 sts, k2tog.

Next row: P2tog, purl to end.

Work 2 more rows in St st, ending with a WS row.

Bind off rem 4 (5:5:6:7) sts.

Transfer center 6 (6:8:8:8) sts to a holder.

With RS facing, rejoin yarn to rem sts, knit to end. [7 (8:8:9:10) sts.]

Next row: Purl to last 2 sts, p2tog.

Next row: K2tog, knit to end.

Next row: Purl to last 2 sts, p2tog.

Work 2 more rows in st st, ending with a WS row.

Bind off rem 4 (5:5:6:7) sts.

FINISHING

Press both pieces carefully. Join right shoulder seam.

Neckband

With RS facing, pick up and knit 5 sts down left side of front neck, k6 (6:8:8:8) sts from front, pick up and knit 5 sts up right side of front neck and 2 sts down right side of back neck, k8 (8:10:10:10) sts across the back, pick up and knit 2 sts up left side of back neck. [28 (28:32:32:32) sts.]

Beg with a purl row, work 2 rows in St st.

Bind off.

Join left shoulder seam and neckband. Join side seams.

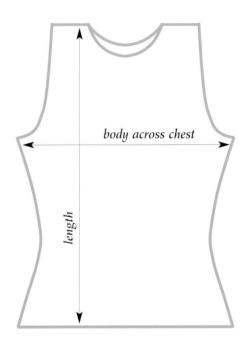

Basic shape for a round-neck tank top.

Polo-neck tank top

This close-fitting and lightweight polo-neck summer top in a ribbon yarn is worked in stockinette stitch. When knitted on large needles, the tape creates a springy and stretchy fabric.

Estimated time of project: 6 hours

Measurements
To fit bust:

32	34	36	38	40	in.
81	86	91	97	102	cm

Actual measurements
Body across chest:

16¾	17¾	18¾	19¾	20¾	in.
42.5	45	47.5	50	52.5	cm

Length:

20½	21¼	21¾	22½	22¾	in.
52	54	55	57	58	cm

The pattern gives the number of stitches for the smallest size; larger sizes follow in brackets.

MATERIALS
3 (3:3:4:4) balls of Jaeger Celeste tape in Shrimp
Pair of 15 mm (US 19) needles

GAUGE
8 stitches and 10 rows to 4 in. (10 cm) measured over stockinette stitch using US 19 (15 mm) needles.

BACK
Cast on 32 (34:36:38:40) sts using US 19 (15 mm) needles.
Beg with a knit row, work in St st.

Shape waist
Dec 1 st at each end of 7th and following 4th row.
[28 (30:32:34:36) sts.]
Work 7 (7:7:9:9) rows, ending with a WS row.
Inc 1 st at each end of next row and every foll 4th row until there are 34 (36:38:40:42) sts.
Cont to work without shaping until work measures 11¾ (12¼:12½:13:13½) in. (30 (31:32:33:34) cm).

Shape armholes
Bind off 2 sts at beg of next 2 rows.
[30 (32:34:36:38) sts.]
Dec 1 st at each end of next row and foll alt row.
[26 (28:30:32:34) sts.]
Cont without shaping until armhole measures 8 (8¼:8¼:8¾:8¾) in. (20 (21:21:22:22) cm), ending with a WS row.

Shape back neck
Work each side of neck separately.
Next row: K9 (10:10:11:12) sts and turn, leaving rem sts on a holder.

This unusual yarn produces an open-textured fabric.

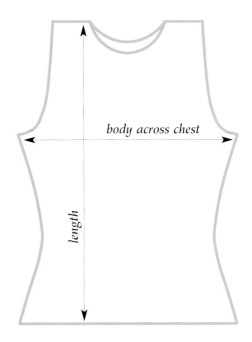

body across chest

length

Basic shape for a polo-neck tank top.

Next row: Dec 1 st at beg of row. [8 (9:9:10:11) sts.]
Bind off rem 8 (9:9:10:11) sts.
Transfer center 8 (8:10:10:10) sts to a holder.
With RS facing, rejoin yarn to rem sts, knit to end.
[9 (10:10:11:12) sts.]
Next row: Dec 1 st at end of row. [8 (9:9:10:11) sts.]
Bind off rem 8 (9:9:10:11) sts.

FRONT
Work as for back until 4 rows less have been worked
to beg of neck shaping, ending with a WS row.

Shape neck
Work each side of neck separately.
Next row: K11 (12:12:13:14) sts and turn, leaving rem
sts on a holder.
Next row: P2tog, purl to end of row.
Next row: Knit to last 2 sts, k2tog.
Next row: P2tog, purl to end of row.
Work 2 more rows in st st, ending with a WS row.
Bind off rem 8 (9:9:10:11) sts.
Transfer center 4 (4:6:6:6) sts to a holder.

With RS facing, rejoin yarn to rem sts, knit to end.
Next row: Purl to last 2 sts, p2tog.
Next row: K2tog, knit to end.
Next row: Purl to last 2 sts, p2tog.
Work 2 more rows in st st, ending with a WS row.
Bind off rem 8 (9:9:10:11) sts.

FINISHING
Press all pieces carefully. Join right shoulder seam.

Polo neck
With RS facing, pick up and knit 7 sts down left side of
front neck, k4 (4:6:6:6) sts across front, pick up and
knit 7 sts up right side of front neck and 4 sts down
right side of back neck, k8 (8:10:10:10) sts across back,
pick up and knit 4 sts up left side of back neck.
[34 (34:38:38:38) sts.]
Beg with a knit row, work in rev St st until neck
measures 8 in. (20 cm), ending with a WS row. Bind off.
When the neck is folded over the knit side will be on
the outside.
Sew polo neck and left shoulder seam. Join side seams.

Skill rating:
Easy

Hooded top

This simple knitted top is worked throughout in stockinette stitch with minimal shaping and casual drop-down shoulders to create an easy-to-wear, loose-fitting feel. Instead of cuffs and edgings, the fabric will naturally curl up to create a rolled edge.

Estimated time of project: 8½ hours

Measurements
To fit bust:

32	34	36	38	40	in.
81	86	91	97	102	cm

Actual measurements
Body across chest:

16¼	17¼	18¼	19½	20½	in.
41.5	44	46.5	49.5	52	cm

Length:

19	19¾	20½	21¼	22	in.
48	50	52	54	56	cm

Sleeves (measured from underarm to sleeve):

17¼	17¼	17¼	18	18	in.
44	44	44	46	46	cm

The pattern gives the number of stitches for the smallest size first; larger sizes follow in brackets.

MATERIALS
6 (6:7:7: 8) balls of Rowan Big Wool in Smoky
Two pairs of US 19 (15 mm) needles

GAUGE
7½ stitches and 10 rows to 4 in. (10 cm) measured over stockinette stitch using US 19 (15 mm) needles.

BACK
Cast on 31 (33:35:37:39) sts using US 19 (15 mm) needles.
Beg with a knit row, work in St st until work measures 19 (19¾:20½:21¼:22) in. (48 (50:52:54:56) cm), ending with a WS row.

Shape back neck and shoulders
Bind off 10 (11:12:12:13) sts at beg of next 2 rows.
Transfer rem 11 (11:11:13:13) sts to a holder.

FRONT
Work until front measures 4 rows less than back to beg of shoulder shaping, ending with a WS row.

Shape neck and shoulders (left side)
Work each side of neck separately.
Next row: K13 (13:13:15:15) sts and turn, leaving rem sts on a holder.
Dec 1 st at neck edge of next and foll row.
[11 (11:11:13:13) sts.]
Work 1 row.
Bind off rem sts.

THREE-NEEDLE BIND OFF

This method is used for creating a seamless join when the number of stitches on each edge is equal. With the right sides facing inwards, hold both needles in the left hand. With the right hand and a third needle, *work into the first stitch on both needles. Work a second stitch as the first; slip the first stitch over the second. * Repeat from *.

Shape neck and shoulders (right side)

With RS facing rejoin yarn to rem sts. Bind off center 5 (7:9:7:9) sts, knit to end. [13 (13:13:15:15) sts.]
Dec 1 st at neck edge of next and foll row.
[11 (11:11:11:13) sts.]
Work 1 row.
Bind off rem sts.

SLEEVES (make 2)

Cast on 21 (21:21:23:23) sts using US 19 (15 mm) needles.
Beg with a knit row, work in St st and shape sides by inc 1 st at each end of 9th row and every foll 8th row until there are 29 (29:31:31:33) sts.
Cont without shaping until sleeve measures 17¼ (17¼:17¼:18:18) in. (44 (44:44:46:46) cm), ending with a WS row.

HOOD

Press both the front and back of the body and join shoulder seams.
With RS facing, pick up and knit 24 (24:24:26:26) sts evenly around the neck, starting at the right side of neck and leaving center 5 (7:7:7:9) sts at front free.
Beg with a purl row, work 5 rows in St st, ending with a WS row.
Next row: *K3, inc in next st,* rep from * to * 4 (4:4:5:5) times more, k4 (4:4:2:2).
[29 (29:29:32:32) sts.]
Next row: Purl.
Next row: *K4, inc in next st * rep from * to * 4 (4:4:5:5) times more, k4 (4:4:2:2).
[34 (34:34:38:38) sts.]
Next row: Purl.
Next row: *K5, inc in next st * rep from * to * 4 (4:4:5:5) times more, k4 (4:4:2:2).
[39 (39:39:44:44) sts.]
Next row: Purl.
Next row: *K6, inc in next st * rep from * to * 4 (4:4:5:5) times more, k4 (4:4:2:2).
[44 (44:44:50:50) sts.]
Cont without shaping until hood measures 30 (30:30:32:32) cm (11¾ (11¾:11¾:12½:12½) in), ending with a WS row.

Put half the sts on one needle and half on another needle. With right sides facing and beginning at the front edge of the hood, bind off using the three-needle bind-off method.

FINISHING

Pin the sleeves in place at the shoulders, ensuring that the underarm is at the same height on both sides of the body. Sew in the sleeves. Join side and sleeve seams.

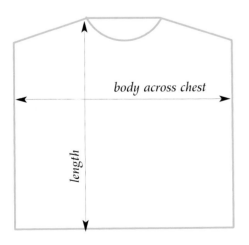

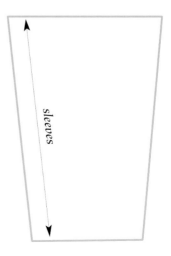

Basic shapes for a hooded top.

Skill rating:
Easy

Chenille vest with fur trim

This cosy winter warmer is made to be loose-fitting and can be worn over a sweater or jacket. Quick and easy to make, it is worked throughout in stockinette stitch in a chunky chenille and trimmed with a fur-like yarn knitted around the edges.

Estimated time of project: 7 hours

Measurements
To fit bust:

32	34	36	38	40	in.
81	86	91	97	102	cm

Actual measurements
Body across chest:

18½	19¾	20¾	22½	23½	in.
47	50	53	57	60	cm

Length:

21¼	21¾	22½	22	23½	in.
54	55	57	58	60	cm

The pattern gives the number of stitches for the smallest size first; larger sizes follow in brackets.

MATERIALS
3 (3:4:4:4) balls of Sirdar Wow in Black
3 (3:3:3:4) balls of Jaeger Fur in Ocelot
Pair of US 15 (10 mm) needles
US N (9 mm) crochet hook (optional)
Chenille needle or length of smooth yarn to match the main body color for sewing up

GAUGE
6 stitches and 10 rows to 4 in. (10 cm) measured over stockinette stitch using US 15 (10 mm) needles and Sirdar Wow.

BACK
Using chenille yarn, cast on 28 (30:32:34:36) sts using US 15 (10 mm) needles.
Beg with a knit row, work in St st until work measures 12¼ (12½:13:13½:13¾) in. (31 (32:33:34:35) cm), ending with a WS row.

Shape armholes
Bind off 3 sts at beg of next 2 rows.
[22 (24:26:28:30) sts.]
Dec 1 st at each end of next row. [20 (22, 24, 26, 28) sts.]
Cont without shaping until armhole measures 7¾ (7¾:8¼:8¼:8½) in. (20 (20:21:21:22) cm), ending with a WS row.

TIPS

The chenille may seem stiff when casting on. Make sure you don't pull the yarn too tightly, as this will pucker the fabric. Instead keep the stitches nice and loose. Remember, you will be adding trimming to the cast-on edge.

The fur trim adds extra warmth to this chic vest.

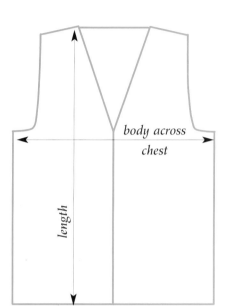

Basic shape for a chenille vest.

Shape shoulders
Bind off 3 sts at beg of next 2 rows.
Bind off 3 (3:4:4:5) sts at beg of following 2 rows.
Bind off rem 8 (10:10:12:12) sts.

LEFT FRONT
Using chenille yarn, cast on 14 (15:16:17:18) sts using US 15 (10 mm) needles.
Beg with a knit row, work in St st until left front matches back to beg of armhole shaping, ending with a WS row.

Shape neck and armholes
Next row: Bind off 3 sts, knit to last 2 sts, k2tog. [10 (11:12:13:14) sts.]
Work 1 row.
Dec 1 st at each end of next row.
Work 1 row.
Dec 1 st at the neck edge of next and every foll alt row until 6 (6:7:7:8) sts rem.
Cont without shaping until armhole matches back to beg of shoulder shaping, ending with a WS row.

Shape shoulders
Bind off 3 sts at beg of next row.
Work 1 row.
Bind off rem 3 (3:4:4:5) sts.

RIGHT FRONT
Using chenille yarn, cast on 14 (15:16:17:18) sts using US 15 (10 mm) needles.
Beg with a knit row, work in St st until right front matches back to beg of armhole shaping, ending with a RS row.

Shape neck and armhole
Bind off 3 st at beg of next row.
Dec 1 st at beg of next row. [10 (11:12:13:14) sts.]
Dec 1 st at each end of next row. [8 (9:10:11:12) sts.]
Work 1 row.
Dec 1 st at the neck edge of next and every foll alt row until 6 (6:7:7:8) sts rem.
Cont without shaping until armhole matches back to beg of shoulder shaping, ending with a RS row.

Shape shoulder
Bind off 3 sts at beg of next row.
Work 1 row.
Bind off rem 3 (3:4:4:5) sts.

FINISHING
When sewing seams you should use either a chenille needle, which is sharper and has a larger eye than a tapestry needle, or a smooth yarn of the same color because the chenille has a tendency to disintegrate when used in sewing.

Armhole trim (both alike)
Join shoulder seams. Using Fur yarn and with RS facing, start at underarm edge and pick up and knit 1 st in each st and 1 st in each row end. Bind off.

Body trim
Back: Join side seams using mattress stitch. Using Fur yarn and with RS facing, attach yarn at left bottom edge and pick up and knit 1 st in every st along the bottom. Bind off.
Front: Working each side separately, using Fur yarn and with RS facing, start at bottom of front opening and pick up and knit 1 st in every st or row end until center of back neck. Bind off. Join at the center of back neck.

Crochet trim
You may prefer to crochet the fur trim instead of knitting it. Using a US N (9 mm) hook, double crochet 1 st into each st and each row end, working 2 rows around the armholes and 2 rows along the bottom edge and around the front opening.

Skill rating: *Easy*

Short round-neck cardigan

This round-neck short cardigan is worked mainly in stockinette stitch. The shape is straight and boxy, so minimal shaping is required. It is edged in a contrasting stitch for definition. Ideal for wearing over an evening dress, the sides of the cardigan are shallow, so it can be worn with a single button or tie at the neck.

Estimated time of project: 7½ hours

Measurements
To fit bust:

32	34	36	38	40	in.
81	86	91	97	102	cm

Actual measurements
Body across chest:

14½	15¾	16¾	18	19	in.
37.5	40	42.5	45.5	48	cm

Length:

17¾	17¾	19	19	19¾	in.
45	45	48	48	50	cm

Sleeves (measured from underarm to wrist):

17½	17½	17½	18	18	in.
44	44	44	46	46	cm

The pattern gives the number of stitches for the smallest size first; larger sizes follow in brackets.

MATERIALS
5 (5:6:7:8) balls of Rowan Big Wool in Bohemian
Pair of US 19 (15 mm) needles
1 button
Sewing needle and matching thread to attach button

GAUGE
7½ stitches and 10 rows to 4 in. (10 cm) measured over stockinette stitch using US 19 (15 mm) needles.

BACK
Cast on 28 (30:32:34:36) sts using US 19 (15 mm) needles.
Beg with a purl row, work in rev St st for 3 rows.
Beg with a purl row, work in St st.
Cont until work measures 10¼ (10¼:10½:10½:11¼) in. (26 (26:27:27:28) cm), ending with a WS row.

Shape armholes
Bind off 2 sts at beg of next 2 rows.
[24 (26:28:30:32) sts.]
Dec 1 st at each end of next row.
[22 (24:26:28:30) sts.]
Cont until armhole measures 7½ (7½:8¼:8¼:8¾) in. (19 (19:21:21:22) cm), ending with a WS row.

The edge stitching is slightly different than that of the body.

Shape shoulders
Bind off 3 sts at beg of next 2 rows.
Bind off 3 (4:5:5:6) sts at beg of following 2 rows.
Bind off rem 10 (10:10:12:12) sts.

LEFT FRONT
Cast on 14 (15:16:17:18) sts using US 19 (15 mm) needles.
Beg with a purl row, work in rev St st for 3 rows.
Beg with a purl row, work in St st with a rev st st border at the front opening as follows:
Row 1 (WS): K3, purl to end.
Row 2 (RS): Knit to last 3 sts, p3.
Repeat rows 1 and 2 until front matches back to beg of armhole shaping, ending with a WS row.

Shape armhole
Bind off 2 sts at beg of next row.
[12 (13:14:15:16) sts.]
Work 1 row.
Dec 1 st at beg of next row. [11 (12:13:14:15) sts.]
Cont to work without shaping until 12 rows less than the back have been worked to beg of shoulder shaping, ending with a WS row.
Next row: Knit to last 4 sts, p4.
Next row: K5, purl to end.
Next row: Knit to last 6 sts, p6.

Shape neck
Work the neck shaping inside the rev St st border as follows:
Bind off 3 (3:3:4:4) sts at beg of next row (neck edge), p3, knit to end.
Next row: Knit to last 3 sts, p3.
Next row: K3, p2tog, purl to end.
Next row: Knit to last 5 sts, k2tog, p3.
[6 (7:8:8:9) sts.]
Work 5 rows in St st with rev St st border without shaping, ending with a WS row.

Shape shoulder
Bind off 3 sts at beg of next row.
Work 1 row.
Bind off rem 3 (4:5:5:6) sts.

RIGHT FRONT
Cast on 14 (15:16:17:18) sts using US 19 (15 mm) needles.
Beg with a purl row, work in rev St st for 3 rows.
Beg with a purl row, work in St st with a rev St st border at the front opening as follows:
Row 1 (WS): Purl to last 3 sts, k3.
Row 2 (RS): P3, knit to end.
Repeat rows 1 and 2 until front matches back to beg of armhole shaping, ending with a RS row.

Shape armhole
Bind off 2 sts at beg of next row.
[12 (13:14:15:16) sts.]
Dec 1 st at end of next row. [11 (12:13:14:15) sts.]
Cont to work without shaping until 11 rows less than the back have been worked to beg of shoulder shaping, ending with a RS row.
Next row: Purl to last sts, k4.

Next row: P5, knit to end.
Next row: Purl to last 6 sts, k6.

Shape neck
Work the neck shaping inside the rev St st border as follows:
Bind off 3 (3:3:4:4) sts at beg of next row (neck edge), p3, knit to end.
Next row: Purl to last 3 sts, k3.
Next row: P3, k2tog, knit to end.
Next row: Purl to last 5 sts, p2tog, k3.
[6 (7:8:8:9) sts.]
Work 5 rows in St st with rev St st border without shaping, ending with a RS row.

Shape shoulder
Bind off 3 sts at beg of next row.
Work 1 row.
Bind off rem 3 (4:5:5:6) sts.

SLEEVES (make 2)
Cast on 19 (19:19:21:21) sts using 15 mm (US 19 needles).
Beg with a purl row, work in rev St st for 3 rows.
Beg with a purl row, work in St st and shape sides by inc 1 st at each end of 6th and every foll 10th (10th:8th:10th:8th) row until there are 27 (27:29:29:31) sts.
Work 5 (5:3:7:5) more rows, ending with a WS row.

Shape top of sleeve
Bind off 2 sts at beg of next 2 rows.
[23 (23:25:25:27) sts.]
Dec 1 st at each end of next and foll 3 alt rows.
[15 (15:17:17:19) sts.]
Dec 1 st at each end of foll 3 (3:3:3:5) rows, ending with a WS row.
Bind off rem 9 (9:11:11:9) sts.

FINISHING
Press all pieces carefully. Join shoulder seams. Join side seams. Join sleeve seams. Insert sleeves. Sew on button. No buttonhole is needed; the button will slip easily through the fabric.

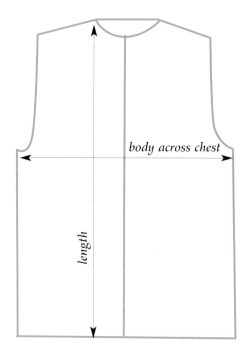

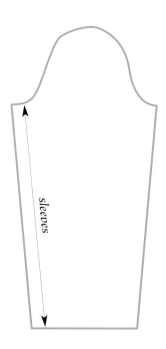

Basic shapes for a short round-neck cardigan.

Skill rating:
Medium

Belt-tie cardigan with collar

A relaxed and easy-to-wear cardigan that does away with zippers and buttons and uses a simple belt that ties at the waist. It is worked throughout in stockinette stitch, with deep ribbing at the cuffs and bottom edge and a wide collar.

Estimated time of project: 12 hours

Measurements
To fit bust:

32	34	36	38	40	in.
81	86	91	97	102	cm

Actual measurements
Body across chest:

16¾	18	19	20	21	in.
42.5	45.5	48	50.5	53.5	cm

Length:

23½	24	24¾	25	26	in.
60	61	63	64	66	cm

Sleeves (measured from underarm to wrist):

17	17	17¼	17¼	17¾	in.
43	43	44	44	45	cm

The pattern gives the number of stitches for the smallest size first; larger sizes follow in brackets.

MATERIALS
8 (8:9:9:10) balls of Rowan Big Wool in Pip
Pair of US 17 (12 mm) needles
Pair of US 19 (15 mm) needles

GAUGE
7½ stitches and 10 rows to 4 in. (10 cm) measured over stockinette stitch using US 19 (15 mm) needles.

BACK
Cast on 36 (38:40:42:44) sts using US 17 (12 mm) needles.
Work in 2 x 2 rib:
Row 1 (RS): *k2, p2 * rep patt from * to last 0 (2:0:2:0) sts, k0 (2:0:2:0).
Row 2 (WS): P0 (2:0:2:0) *k2, p2 * rep patt from *.
Working in rib, rep rows 1 and 2 five more times ending with a WS row.
Change to US 19 (15 mm) needles. Beg with a knit row, work in St st. Dec 1 st at each end of 3rd and foll 4th row. [32 (34:36:38:40) sts.]
Cont to work in St st until work measures 15¾ (16:16½:17:17¼) in. (40 (41:42:43:44) cm), ending with a WS row.

Shape armholes
Bind off 2 sts at beg of next 2 rows.
[28 (30:32:34:36) sts.]
Dec 1 st at each end of next row.
[26 (28:30:32:34) sts.]

Cont without shaping until armhole measures 7¾ (7¾:8¼:8¼:8½) in. (20 (20:21:21:22) cm), ending with a WS row.

Shape shoulders
Bind off 4 sts at beg of next 2 rows.
Bind off 5 (5:5:6:6) sts at beg of foll 2 rows.
Transfer rem 8 (10:12:12:14) sts to a holder.

LEFT FRONT
Cast on 20 (21:22:23:24) sts using US 17 (12 mm) needles.
Work in 2 x 2 rib:
Row 1 (RS): P0 (2:0:2:0) *k2, p2 * rep patt from * to last 0 (3:2:1:0) sts, k0 (2:2:1:0), p0 (1:0:0:0).
Row 2 (WS): K0 (1:0:0:0), p0 (2:2:1:0) *k2, p2 * rep patt from * to last 0 (2:0:2:0) sts, k0 (2:0:2:0).
Rep rows 1 and 2 five more times, ending with a WS row.
Change to US 19 (15 mm) needles. You will be working in St st with a g st selvedge at the front opening.
Next row: Knit.
Next row: K1, purl to end.
Follow patt as set.
Dec 1 st at beg of 3rd row (from beg of patt) and foll 4th row. [18 (19:20:21:22) sts.]
Cont to work in St st with g st selvedge until front matches back to beg of armhole shaping, ending with a WS row.

Shape armhole
Bind off 2 sts at beg of next row.
[16 (17:18:19:20) sts.]
Cont to work g st selvedge until you reach neck shaping.
Work 1 row.
Dec 1 st at beg of next row. [15 (16:17:18:19) sts.]
Cont working in St st until work measures 5 rows less than back to start of shoulder shaping, ending with a RS row.

Shape neck
Bind off 3 (4:5:5:6) sts at beg of next row (neck edge).
[12 (12:12:13:13) sts.]
Dec 1 at neck edge of foll 3 rows.
[9 (9:9:10:10) sts.]
Work 1 row, ending with a WS row.

The wide collar adds extra warmth around the neck.

Shape shoulder
Bind off 4 sts at beg of next row.
Work 1 row.
Bind off rem 5 (5:5:6:6) sts.

RIGHT FRONT
Cast on 20 (21:22:23:24) sts using US 17 (12 mm) needles.
Work in 2 x 2 rib:
Row 1 (RS): K0 (0:0:1:0) p0 (1:2:2:0), *k2, p2 * rep patt from *.
Row 2 (WS): *K2, p2 * rep patt from * to last 0 (1:2:3:0) sts, k0 (1:2:2:0), p0 (0:0:1:0).
Rep rows 1 and 2 five more times, ending with a WS row.

Change to US 19 (15 mm) needles. You will be working in St st with a g st selvedge at the front opening.
Next row: Knit.
Next row: Purl to last st, k1.
Follow patt as set.
Dec 1 st at end of 3rd row (from beg of patt) and foll 4th row. [18 (19, 20, 21, 22) sts.]

Cont to work in St st with g st selvedge until right front matches back to beg of armhole shaping, ending with a RS row.

Shape armhole

Bind off 2 sts at beg of next row.
[16 (17:18:19:20) sts.]
Cont to work g st selvedge until you reach neck shaping.
Dec 1 st at end of next of row. [15 (16:17:18:19) sts.]
Cont working in St st until work measures 6 rows less than back to start of shoulder shaping, ending with a WS row.

Shape neck

Bind off 3 (4:5:5:6) sts at beg of next row (neck edge).
[12 (12:12:13:13) sts.]
Dec 1 st at neck edge of foll 3 rows.
[9 (9:9:10:10) sts.]
Work 3 rows, ending with a RS row.

Shape shoulder

Bind off 4 sts at beg of next row.
Work 1 row.
Bind off rem 5 (5:5:6: 6) sts.

SLEEVES (make 2)

Cast on 21 (21:21:23:23) sts using 12 mm (US 17) needles.
Work in 2 x 2 rib to create a cuff:
Row 1 (RS): P1 (1:1:2:2) *k2, p2*, rep patt from * to last 0 (0:0:1:1) st, p0 (0:0:1:1).
Row 2 (WS): K0 (0:0:1:1) *k2, p2*, rep patt from * to last 1 (1:1:2:2) sts, k1 (1:1:2:2).
Rep rows 1 and 2, five more times, ending with a WS row.
Change to US 19 (15 mm) needles. Beg with a knit row, work in St st and shape sides by inc 1 st at each end of 5th and every foll 8th row until there are 27 (27:29:29:31) sts.
Cont without shaping until sleeve measures 17 (17:17¼:17¼:17¾) in. (43 (43:44:44:45) cm), ending with a WS row.

Shape top of sleeve

Bind off 2 sts at beg of next 2 rows.
[23 (23:25:25: 27) sts.]
Dec 1 st at each end of next and foll 5 (5:5:5:6) alt rows. [11 (11:13:13:13) sts.]
Work 1 row.
Dec 1 st at each end of next 2 (2:3:3:3) rows.
Work 0 (0:1:1:1) row, ending with a WS row.
Bind off rem 7 sts.

FINISHING

Press all pieces, avoiding ribbing. Join shoulder seams.

Collar

With RS facing, using US 17 (12 mm) needles, pick up and knit 10 sts up the right side of the neck, k8 (10:12:12:14) sts across the back, pick up and knit 10 sts down the left side of the neck.
[28 (30:32:32:34) sts.]
Work in 2 x 2 rib:
Row 1: P0 (2: 0: 0: 2) *k2, p2 * rep patt from *.
Row 2: *k2, p2* rep patt from * to last 0 (2: 0: 2: 0) sts, k0 (2: 0: 0: 2).
Cont to work in rib until collar measures 8 in. (20 cm), ending with a WS row. Bind off in rib.

Matching center of sleeve to shoulder seam and sleeve edge to underarm, sew sleeves in place. Join side and sleeve seams.

Make belt loops by taking a length of yarn and sewing the ends into each side seam at waist height.

Belt

The belt can be any length you want it to be; it depends on whether you prefer long or short tails hanging down. The belt will naturally curl so that it appears to be a long tube.
Cast on 4 sts using US 17 (12 mm) needles.
Beg with a knit row, work in St st until belt reaches desired length. Bind off.

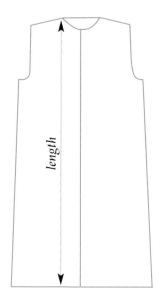

Basic shapes for a belt-tie cardigan with a collar.

Skill rating:
Medium

Long cardigan coat

This is a long, subtly shaped knitted cardigan that buttons up the front and has pockets on either side. It has simple flowing lines and is edged in seed stitch at the cuffs, hem, and side borders to give it definition.

Estimated time of project: 15 hours

Measurements
To fit bust:

32	34	36	38	40	in.
81	86	91	97	102	cm

Actual measurements
Body across chest:

16¼	17¼	18¼	19¼	20¼	in.
41	44	46	49	51	cm

Length:

38½	39¼	39¾	40½	41	in.
98	100	101	103	104	cm

Sleeves (measured from underarm to wrist):

18½	18½	19	19	19¼	in.
47	47	48	48	49	cm

The pattern gives the number of stitches for the smallest size first; larger sizes follow in brackets.

MATERIALS
11 (11:12:12:13) balls of Rowan Big Wool in Wild Berry
Pair of US 17 (12 mm) needles
6 large buttons
Sewing needle and matching thread to attach buttons

GAUGE
8 stitches and 12 rows to 4 in. (10 cm) measured over stockinette stitch using US 17 (12 mm) needles.

BACK
Cast on 43 (45:47:49:51) sts using US 17 (12 mm) needles.
Work in seed stitch for 8 rows as follows:
Row 1: *K1, p1*, rep from * to last st, k1.
Rep row 1 seven times more.
Beg with a knit row (right side), work in st st.
Dec 1 st at each end of 17th and every foll 16th row until 33 (35:37:39:41) sts remain.
Cont to work without shaping until work measures 31 (31½:32:32¼:32¾) in. (79 (80:81:82:83) cm), ending with a WS row.

Shape armholes
Bind off 2 sts at beg of next 2 rows.
[29 (31:33:35:37) sts.]
Dec 1 st at each end of next and foll alt row.
[25 (27:29:31:33) sts.]
Cont straight until armhole measures 7½ (8:8:8¼:8¼) in. (19 (20:20:21:21) cm), ending with a WS row.

Shape shoulders

Bind off 3 sts at beg of next 2 rows.
Bind off 4 (5:5:6:6) sts at beg of next 2 rows.
Bind off rem 11 (11:13:13:15) sts.

LEFT FRONT

Cast on 22 (23:24:25:26) sts using US 17 (12 mm) needles.
Work in seed stitch for 8 rows as follows:
Row 1: *K1, p1 * rep from * to last 0 (1:0:1:0) st, k0 (1:0:1:0).
Row 2: P1 (0: 1: 0: 1) *k1, p1 *, rep from * to last st, k1.
Rep rows 1 and 2 three times more.
Beg with a knit row (right side), work in St st.
Dec 1 st at beg of 17th and every foll 16th row until work measures 19¾ in. (50 cm), ending with a WS row.

Pocket

Creates a pocket top with seed stitch edging.
Next row: K5 (5:6:6:7), *k1, p1* rep from * 4 times more, knit to end.
Next row: P4 (5:5:6:6) *k1, p1* rep from * 4 times more, purl to end.
Rep last 2 rows twice more.
Follow instructions for inserting a pocket (see page 81). Remember to continue to dec 1 st at beg of every

foll 16th row while inserting the pocket until 17 (18:19:20:21) sts rem.

Cont to work without shaping until left front matches back to beg of armhole shaping, ending with a WS row.

Shape neck and armhole

Bind off 2 sts at beg and dec 1 st at the end (neck edge) of next row.
Work 1 row.
Next row: Dec 1 st at each end of row.
Work 1 row.
Next row: Dec 1 st at each end of row.
Work 1 row.
Dec 1 st at neck edge only on next and every foll alt row until 7 (8:8:9:9) sts rem.

Cont without shaping until left front matches back to beg of shoulder shaping, ending with a WS row.

Shape shoulder

Bind off 3 sts at beg of next row.
Work 1 row.
Bind off rem 4 (5:5:6:6) sts.

RIGHT FRONT

Cast on 22 (23:24:25:26) sts using US 17 (12 mm) needles.
Work in seed stitch for 8 rows as follows.
Row 1: *K1, p1* rep from * to last 0 (1:0:1:0) sts, k0 (1:0:1:0).
Row 2: P1 (0:1:0:1) *k1, p1 *, rep from * to last st, k1.
Rep rows 1 and 2 three times more.
Beg with a knit row (right side), work in St st.
Dec 1 st at end of 17th and every foll 16th row until work measures 19¾ in. (50 cm) ending with a RS row

Pocket

Creates a pocket top with seed stitch edging.
Next row: P5 (5:6:6:7), *k1, p1* rep from * 4 times more, knit to end.
Next row: K4 (5:5:6:6) *k1, p1* rep from * 4 times more, purl to end.
Rep last 2 rows twice more.
Follow instructions for inserting a pocket.
Remember to continue to dec 1 st at end of foll 16th row while inserting the pocket until 17 (18:19:20:21) sts remain.

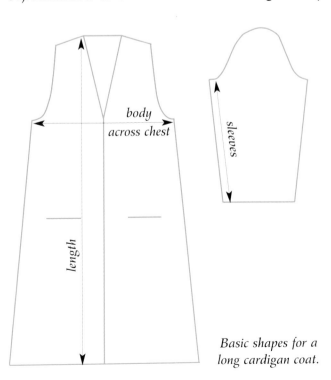

Basic shapes for a long cardigan coat.

Cont to work without shaping until right front matches back to beg of armhole shaping, ending with a WS row.

Shape neck and armhole
Dec 1 st at beg (neck edge) of next row.
Next row: Bind off 2 sts at beg of row.
Next row: Dec 1 st at each end of row.
Work 1 row.
Next row: Dec 1 st at each end of row.
Work 1 row.
Dec 1 st at neck edge only on next and every foll alt row until 7 (8:8:9:9) sts rem.

Cont without shaping until right front matches back to beg of shoulder shaping, ending with a RS row.

Shape shoulder
Bind off 3 sts at beg of next row.
Work 1 row.
Bind off rem 4 (5:5:6:6) sts.

SLEEVES (make 2)
Cast on 25 (25:25:27:27) sts using US 17 (12 mm) needles.
Work in seed stitch for 8 rows as follows:
Row 1: *k1, p1*, rep from * to last st, k1.
Rep row 1 seven times more.
Beg with a knit row, work in st st and shape sides by inc 1 st at each end of 17th row and foll 18th row. [29 (29:29:31:31) sts.]
Cont without shaping until sleeve measures 18½ (18½:19:19:19¼) in. (47 (47:48:48:49) cm), ending with a WS row.

Shape top of sleeve
Bind off 2 sts at beg of next 2 rows.
[25 (25:25:27:27) sts.]
Dec 1 st at each end of next and every foll alt row until 7 sts rem, ending with a WS row.
Bind off rem 7 sts.

FINISHING
Press all pieces carefully. Join shoulder seams. Set sleeves into armhole shapings. Join side seams. Join sleeve seams.
Sew up the three sides of the pocket lining to the inside of the garment.
Use pins to mark on the front where you will place

INSERTING POCKETS

To make a horizontal pocket, work up to the point where you would like the opening of the pocket to be. On a right side row, bind off pocket stitches (remember to bind off in seed stitch) and continue to work row until the end.

On a new needle, cast on as many stitches as you bind off, adding four stitches to make the pocket edges.

Work in stockinette stitch until pocket lining measures 6 in. (12 cm) ending with a knit row. Bind off two stitches at beginning of next two rows. Break yarn.

To attach the pocket, work 1 row in purl across garment, across pocket lining and to the end of the garment. The pocket lining is now attached to the garment.

---

the buttons, spacing the buttons evenly starting just below the neck shaping.

Button band
This band will carry the buttonholes and buttons on either side of the front opening. The band is knit separately and sewn on.
Using US 17 (12 mm) needles, cast on 5 sts.
Work in seed stitch as follows:
Every row: *K1, p1* rep from * once more, k1.
Work one row for every row up the front opening and one row for every st across the back.

Buttonholes
Start at the right front. When the band reaches the point opposite where you've marked where a button should be, insert an eyelet buttonhole as follows:
Next row: K1, p1, YO (this creates a hole), p2tog, k1.
Work the following row in seed stitch as usual.
Work each of the six buttonholes to correspond with where you have placed markers and continue until the band is long enough to edge both sides of the front opening.
Attach the band using mattress stitch. Sew on the buttons.

Loop jacket

This fun and colorful jacket is created using a loop stitch in a variegated yarn. With its short, boxy shape, it can be worn over an evening gown for a dressier look, or more casually, with jeans. Once you have mastered the loop stitch, this jacket is surprisingly easy to knit.

Estimated time of project: 10 hours

Measurements
To fit bust:

32	34	36	38	40	in.
81	86	91	97	102	cm

Actual measurements
Body across chest:

18	19¼	20½	21½	22¾	in.
46	49	52	55	58	cm

Length:

18½	18½	20	20	21¼	in.
47	47	51	51	54	cm

Sleeves (measured from underarm to wrist):

17¾	17¾	18½	18½	18½	in.
45	45	47	47	47	cm

The pattern gives the number of stitches for the smallest size; larger sizes follow in brackets.

MATERIALS
11 (11:12:13:14:15) balls of Colinette Point Five in Fresco
Pair of US 17 (12 mm) needles

GAUGE
6½ stitches and 10 rows to 4 in. (10 cm) measured over loop stitch using US 17 (12 mm) needles.

SPECIAL TERMS
Loop stitch: Row 1 (RS): knit. **Row 2 (WS):** *insert needle into stitch knitwise, wrap yarn round the needle and over two fingers of the left hand, then over the needle again. Draw through two loops and place them back on the left needle. Knit the two loops together through the back* repeat from * to end of row.

BACK
Cast on 30 (32:34:36:38) sts using US 17 (12 mm) needles.
Beg with a knit row (RS), work in loop stitch.
Cont without shaping until work measures
11 (11:11¾:11¾:12½) in. (28 (28:30:30:32) cm), ending with a loop row (WS).

Shape armholes
Bind off 2 sts at beg of next row.
Next row: Bind off 2 sts knitwise, work in loop st (row 2) to end of row.
Dec 1 st at both ends of next and foll alt row.
[22 (24:26:28:30) sts.]
Cont to work in loop st until armhole measures

$7\frac{1}{2}$ ($7\frac{1}{2}$:8:8:$8\frac{1}{2}$) in. (19 (19:21:21:22) cm), ending with
a loop row.
Bind off knitwise.

LEFT FRONT
Cast on 16 (17:18:19:20) sts using US 17 (12 mm)
needles.
Beg with a knit row (RS), work in loop stitch.
Cont without shaping until work measures same as
back to beg of armhole shaping, ending with a loop
row (WS).

Shape armhole and neck
Bind off 2 sts at beg of next row.
Work 1 row in loop st.
Next row: Dec 1 st at beg of row.
Work 1 row in loop st.
Dec 1 st at each end of next row.
[11 (12:13:14:15) sts.]
Work 1 row in loop st.
Dec 1 st at neck edge of next and every foll alt row
until 7 (7:7:8:8) sts rem.
Cont to work in loop st until front matches back to
bound-off edge, ending with a loop row. Bind off.

RIGHT FRONT
Cast on 16 (17:18:19:20) sts using US 17 (12 mm)
needles.
Beg with a knit row (RS), work in loop stitch.
Cont without shaping until work measures same as
back to beg of armhole shaping, ending with a knit
row (RS).

Shape armhole and neck
Next row: Bind off 2 sts knitwise at beg of row, work
in loop st to end of row.
Next row: Dec 1 st at end of row.
Work 1 row in loop st.
Dec 1 st at each end of next row.
[11 (12:13:14:15) sts.]
Work 1 row in loop st.
Dec 1 st at neck edge of next and every foll alt row
until 7 (7:7:8:8) sts remain.
Cont to work in loop st until front matches back to
bound-off edge, ending with a loop row. Bind off.

SLEEVES (make 2)
Cast on 17 (17:19:19:21) sts using US 17 (12 mm)
needles.

Beg with a knit row (RS), work in loop stitch.
Inc 1 st at each end of 9th and every foll 10th row
until there are 23 (23:25:25:27) sts.
Cont in loop st until sleeve measures
$17\frac{3}{4}$ ($17\frac{3}{4}$:$18\frac{1}{2}$:$18\frac{1}{2}$:$18\frac{1}{2}$) in. (45 (45:47:47:47) cm),
ending with a loop row (WS).

Shape top of sleeve
Bind off 2 sts at beg of next row.
Next row: Bind off 2 sts knitwise, work in loop st to
end of row.
Dec 1 st at each end of next and every foll alt row
until 9 sts rem, ending with a knit row.
Next row: Dec 1 st at each end of next (loop) row.
Bind off rem 7 sts.

FINISHING
There is no need to press the pieces, which should
already lie flat, and you do not want to crush the
loops.
With RS facing, join the shoulder seams. For all other
seams you may find it easier to sew the seams with
the WS facing. Sew the sleeves into the armholes. Join
the side and sleeve seams.

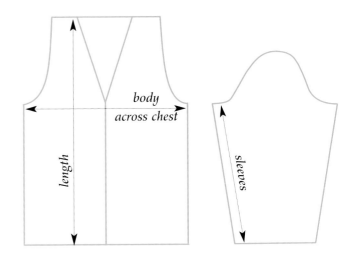

Basic shapes for a loop jacket.

Zip-up jacket

This is a simple unstructured hip-length wool jacket worked in stockinette stitch using chunky wool. Ribbing at the cuffs, collar, and bottom edge adds shape and definition. The front opening fastens with a zipper, leaving an open collar.

Estimated time of project: 10 hours

Measurements
To fit bust:

32	34	36	38	40	in.
81	86	91	97	102	cm

Actual measurements
Body across chest:

17	18	19	19¾	21	in.
43	45.5	48	50.5	53.5	cm

Length:

21¾	21¾	23	23	24	in.
55	55	58	58	61	cm

Sleeves (measured from underarm to wrist):

17¾	17¾	17¾	18	18	in.
45	45	45	46	46	cm

The pattern gives the number of stitches for the smallest size; larger sizes follow in brackets.

MATERIALS
5 (6:6:7:7) balls of Rowan Big Wool in Blue Velvet
Pair of US 17 (12 mm) needles
Pair of US 19 (15 mm) needles
1 separating zipper
Sewing needle and matching thread to attach zipper

GAUGE
7½ stitches and 10 rows to 4 in. (10 cm) measured over stockinette stitch using US 19 (15 mm) needles.

BACK
Cast on 30 (32:34:36:38) sts using US 17 (12 mm) needles.
Work in 2 x 2 rib:
Row 1 (RS): P2 (0:2:0:2) * k2, p2 * rep patt from *.
Row 2 (WS): *K2, p2* rep patt from * to last 2 (0:2:0:2) sts, k2 (0:2:0:2).
Working in rib, rep rows 1 and 2 four times more, ending with a WS row.
Change to US 19 (15 mm) needles.
Beg with a knit row (right side), work in St st.
Next row: Inc 1 st at each end of row.
32 (34:36:38:40) sts.
Cont to work in St st until work measures 13¾ (13¾:14½:14½:15¼) in. (35 (35:37:37:39) cm), ending with a WS row.

Shape armholes
Bind off 2 sts at beg of next 2 rows.
Dec 1 st at each end of next row and foll alt row.
[24 (26:28:30:32) sts.]

The zipper stops just before the collar begins.

Cont until armhole measures 7¾ (7¾:8¼:8¼:8½) in. (20 (20:21:21:22) cm), ending with a WS row.

Shape shoulders
Bind off 4 sts at beg of next 2 rows.
Bind off 4 (5:5:5:6) sts at beg of foll 2 rows.
Bind off rem 8 (8:10:12:12) sts.

LEFT FRONT
Cast on 15 (16:17:18:19) sts using US 17 (12 mm) needles.
Work in 2 x 2 rib:
Row 1 (RS): K1 (0:0:0:1), p2 (0:1:2:2), * k2, p2* rep patt from *.
Row 2 (WS): *K2, p2*. Rep patt from * to last 3 (0:1:2:3) sts, k2 (0:1:2:2), p1 (0:0:0:1).
Rep rows 1 and 2 four times more, ending with a WS row.
Change to US 19 (15 mm) needles.
Beg with a knit row (right side), work in St st.
Next row: Inc 1 st at beg of row.
[16 (17:18:19:20) sts.]
Cont to work in St st until the work matches back to beg of armhole shaping, ending with a WS row.

Shape armhole
Bind off 2 sts at beg of next row.
Work 1 row.
Dec 1 st at beg of next and foll alt row.
[12 (13:14:15:16) sts.]
Cont working in St st until work measures 5 rows less than back to start of shoulder shaping, ending with a RS row.

Shape neck
Bind off 2 (2:2:3:3) sts at beg (neck edge) of next row.
[10 (11:12:12:13) sts.]
Next row: Knit to last 2 sts, k2tog.
Next row: P2tog, purl to end of row.
[8 (9:10:10:11) sts.]

Smallest two sizes
Work 2 rows without shaping, then go to beg of shoulder shaping.

All other sizes
Next row: Knit to last 2 sts, k2tog. [9:9:10 sts.]
Work 1 row.

Shape shoulder
Bind off 4 sts at beg of next row.
Work 1 row.
Bind off rem 4 (5:5:5:6) sts.

RIGHT FRONT
Cast on 15 (16:17:18:19) sts using 12 mm (US 17) needles.
Work in 2 x 2 rib:
Row 1 (RS): *K2, p2 * rep patt from * to last 3 (0:1:2:3) sts, k2 (0:1:2:2), p1 (0:0:0:1).
Row 2 (WS): K1 (0:0:0:1), p2 (0:1:2:2) * k2, p2 *rep patt from * to end.
Rep rows 1 and 2 four times more, ending with a WS row.
Change to US 19 (15 mm) needles.
Beg with a knit row (right side), work in St st.
Next row: Inc 1 st at end of row.
[16 (17:18:19:20) sts.]
Reversing shapings, work as for left front to beg of neck shaping, ending with a WS row.

Shape neck
Bind off 2 (2:2:3:3) sts at beg (neck edge) of next row.
[10 (11:12:12:13) sts.]

Next row: Purl to last 2 sts, p2tog.
Next row: K2tog, knit to end of row.
[8 (9:10:10:11) sts.]

Smallest two sizes
Work 2 rows without shaping, then go to beg of shoulder shaping.

All other sizes
Next row: Purl to last 2 sts, p2tog. [9:9:10 sts.]
Work 1 row.

Shape shoulder
Bind off 4 sts at beg of next row.
Work 1 row.
Bind off rem 4 (5:5:5:6) sts.

SLEEVES (make 2)
Cast on 19 (19:19:21:21) sts using 12 mm (US 17) needles.
Work in 2 x 2 rib to create a cuff:
Row 1 (RS): K1 (1:1:0:0), p2 (2:2:1:1) *k2, p2*, rep patt from * to end.
Row 2 (WS): *K2, p2, *, rep patt from * to last 3 (3:3:1:1) sts, k2 (2:2:1:1), p1 (1:1:0:0).
Rep rows 1 and 2 four times more, ending with a WS row.
Change to 15 mm (US 19) needles.
Beg with a knit row (right side), work in st st and shape sides by inc 1 st at each end of 5th and every foll 8th (8th:6th:8th:6th) row until there are 27 (27:29:29:31) sts.
Cont without shaping until sleeve measures 17¾ (17¾:17¾:18:18) in. (45 (45:45:46:46) cm), ending with a WS row.

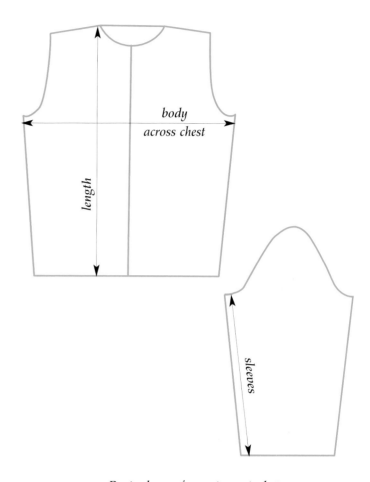

Basic shapes for a zip-up jacket.

Shape top of sleeve
Bind off 2 sts at beg of next 2 rows.
[23 (23:25:25:27) sts.]
Dec 1 st at each end of next and foll 4 (4:4:4:5) alt rows.
Dec 1 st at each end of next 3 (3:4:4:4) rows.
Bind off rem 7 sts.

FINISHING
Press all pieces carefully. Join the shoulder seams.

Collar
Using US 19 (15 mm) needles and with RS facing, pick up and knit 9 (9:10:10:11) sts up right side of neck, 12 (12:14:14:16) sts across the back and 9 (9:10:10:11) sts down left side of neck. [30 (30:34:34:38) sts.]
Work in 2 x 2 rib:
Row 1 (RS): *K2, p2*, rep patt from * to last 2 sts, k2.
Row 2 (WS): *P2, k2*, rep patt from * to last 2 sts, p2.
Cont to work in rib until collar measures 5 in. (12 cm), ending with a WS row. Bind off.

INSERTING THE ZIPPER

Measure the length of the jacket to the start of the collar; this is the length of zipper you will need. With the right side facing, tack together the edges of the front opening. Tack the zipper to the wrong side, so that the teeth are centerd on the opening. On the right side, sew the zipper to the garment using backstitch or alternatively, you can machine-stitch the zipper in place.

Shrug

A shrug is a fun and versatile piece to have in your wardrobe. Essentially, it's a cross between a scarf and a cardigan that is worn around the shoulders. It's up to you how you wear it; you can either dress it up by wearing it over an evening dress, or wear it as you would a cardigan. Straightforward to make, this garment is worked in stockinette stitch. Think of it as a bit like making a shaped scarf, starting at the cuffs, which are worked in rib. To finish it off, the cuffs are sewn together to make sleeves.

Estimated time of project: 5 hours

Measurements
Size:

XS	S	M	L	XL	
52	52¾	54	54¾	56¼	in.
132	134	137	139	143	cm

The measurements given here are for the arm span measured from wrist to wrist. It is worth measuring for the garment first and, if necessary, making any adjustments to the pattern.

MATERIALS
3 (3:3:3:4) balls of Colinette Point Five in Fire
Pair of US 19 (15 mm) needles

GAUGE
7½ stitches and 10 rows to 4 in. (10 cm) measured over stockinette stitch using US 19 (15 mm) needles.

LEFT CUFF
Beg at the cuff, cast on 19 (19:19:21:21) sts using 15 mm (US 19) needles.
Work in 2 x 2 rib to create a cuff:
Row 1 (RS): K1 (1:1:0:0), p2 (2:2:1:1) *k2, p2*, rep patt from *.
Row 2 (WS): *K2, p2, *, rep patt from * to last 3 (3:3:1:1) sts, k2 (2:2:1:1), p1 (1:1:0:0).
Rep rows 1 and 2 four times more, ending with a WS row.

LEFT SLEEVE
Beg with a knit row (right side), work in St st and inc to shape the arm as follows:
Next row: Inc 1 st at beg and end of row.
[21 (21:21:23:23) sts.]
Next row: Purl.

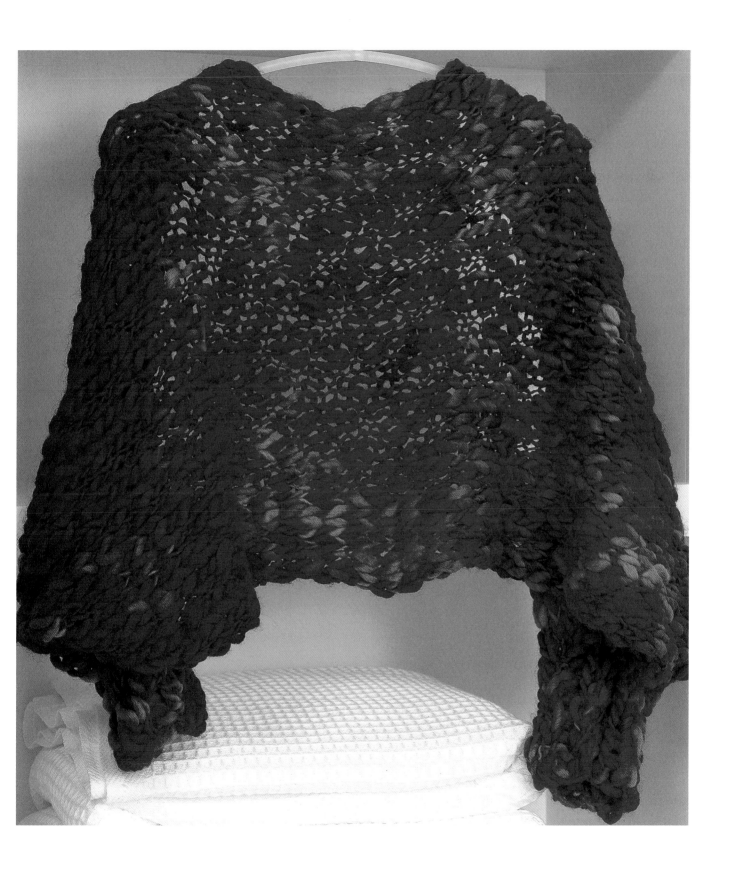

Next row: Inc 1, k5 (5:5:6:6), inc 1, knit to last 7 (7:7:8:8) sts, inc 1, knit to last st, inc 1 st at end of row. [25 (25:25:27:27) sts.]
Next row: Purl.
Next row: Inc 1, k6 (6:6:7:7), inc 1, knit to last 8 (8:8:9:9) sts, inc 1, knit to last st, inc 1 st at end of row. [29 (29:29:31:31) sts.]
Next row: Purl.

BODY
Continue to work in St st ending with a WS (purl) row, until work measures 45¾ (46½:47½:48½:50) in. (116 (118:121:123:127) cm). If you have measured your arm span and found it to be longer than the sizes given here, you can continue until the work measures the length you need, less 6¼ in. (16 cm) for the second arm shaping.

RIGHT SLEEVE
At this point you start to decrease to shape the second sleeve. The shapings are the reverse of the left sleeve.

Next row: K2tog, k7 (7:7:8:8), k2tog, k7 (7:7:8:8), k2tog, k7, k2tog. [25 (25:25:27:27) sts.]
Next row: Purl.
Next row: K2tog, k6, k2tog, k5 (5:5:7:7), k2tog, k6, k2tog. [21 (21:21:23:23) sts.]
Next row: Purl.
Next row: K2tog, knit until the last 2 sts, k2tog. [19 (19:19:21:21) sts.]
Next row: Purl.

RIGHT CUFF
Row 1: *K2, p2, *, rep patt from * to last 3 (3:3:1:1) sts, k2 (2:2:1:1), p1 (1:1:0:0).
Row 2: K1 (1:1:0:0), p2 (2:2: 1:1), *k2, p2*, rep patt from *.
Rep rows 1 and 2 four times more, ending with a WS row. Bind off in patt.

FINISHING
Press carefully, avoiding the ribbing. Sew up the cuffs and sleeves up the first 7¾ (7¾:7¾:8½:8½) in. (20 (20:20:22:22) cm), from the cuff on both sides.

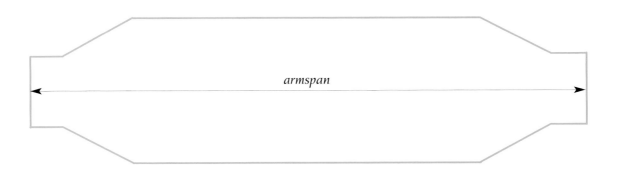

Basic shape for a shrug.

Suppliers

UK

Bobbins
Wesley Hall
Church Street
Whitby
North Yorkshire
YO22 4DE
Tel: (01947) 600585

Colinette Yarns
Banwy Workshops
Llanfair Caereinion
Powy
Wales
SY21 0SG
Tel: (01938) 810128
Fax: (01938) 810127
www.colinette.com

David Morgan Ltd
26 The Hayes
Cardiff
Wales
CF10 1UG
Tel: (029) 2022 1011

Designer Yarns Ltd
Unit 8-10 Newbridge
 Industrial Estate
Pitt Street
Kingly
West Yorkshire
BD21 4PQ
Tel: (01535) 664222

Jaegar Handknits
Green Mill Lane
Holmfirth
West Yorkshire
HD 2DX
Tel: (01484) 680050

Liberty Plc
214 Regent Street
London
W1R 6AH
Tel: (020) 7734 1234

John Lewis
Oxford Street
London
W1A 1EX
Tel: (020) 7629 7711

Rowan Yarns
Green Mill Lane
Holmfirth
West Yorkshire
HD 2DX
Tel: (01484) 681 881
www.rowanyarns.co.uk

**Shoreham Knitting
 and Needlecraft**
9 East Street
Shoreham-by-Sea
West Sussex
BN43 5ZE
Tel: (01273) 461029
Fax: (01273) 465407
www.englishyarns.co.uk

Sirdar Spinning Ltd
Flanshaw Lane
Wakefield
West Yorkshire
WF2 9ND
Tel: (01924) 371501
Fax: (01924) 290506
www.sirdar.co.uk

Stitch Shop
15 The Podium
Northgate
Bath
BA1 5AL
Tel: (01255) 481134

Texere Yarns
College Mill
Barkerend Road
Bradford
West Yorkshire
BD1 4AU
Tel: (01274) 722191
Fax: (01274) 393500
www.texere.co.uk

UNITED STATES

Knitting Fever Inc
35 Debevoise Avenue
Roosevelt, NY 11575
Tel: (516) 546 3600
www.knittingfever.com

Knit Picks
13118 NE 4th St.
Vancouver, WA 98684
Tel: (800) 574 1323
www.knitpicks.com

Patternworks
P.O. Box 1618
Center Harbor, NH 03226
Tel: (800) 723 9210
www.patternworks.com

Rowan USA
4 Townsend West, Suite 8
Nashua, NH 03063
Tel: (603) 886 5041/5043
Email: wfibers@aol.com

Unique Kolours
1428 Oak Lane
Downingtown, PA 19335
Tel: (610) 280 7720
Fax: (610) 280 7701
www.uniquekolours.com

CANADA

Diamond Yarn
155 Martin Ross, Unit 3
Toronto, ON, M3J 2L9
Tel: (416) 736 6111
Fax: (416) 736 6112
www.diamondyarn.com

Ram Wools
1266 Fife Street
Winnipeg, MB, R2X 2N6
Tel: (204) 949 6868
 www.ramwools.com

Yarn information

Colinette Point Five
100% wool
Approximately 54 yds
(50 m) per 50 g skein

Jaeger Celeste
50% viscose, 20% linen,
30% polyamide
Approximately 98 yds
(90 m) per 50 g ball

Jaeger Fur
47% kid mohair, 47% wool,
6% polyamide
Approximately 22 yds
(20 m) per 50 g ball

Rowan Big Wool
100% wool
Approximately 86 yds
(80 m) per 100 g ball

Rowan Biggy Print
100% wool
Approximately 32 yds
(30 m) per 100 g ball

Sirdar Denim Ultra
15% wool, 25% cotton,
60% acrylic)
Approximately 82 yds
(76 m) per 100 g ball

Sirdar Wow!
100% polyester
Approximately 63 yds
(58 m) per 100 g ball

Texere Destiny Mohair
82% mohair, 9% wool,
9% nylon
Approximately 108 yds
(100 m) per 50 g ball

Acknowledgements

Thanks to Tris for not complaining too bitterly about our yarn-strewn house, and for his patience with my false promises of "just one more row," and to Balthazar for largely keeping his claws to himself. Thanks also to my mother for her expert advice and knitting skills.

I would also like to thank my editor, Clare Sayer, for turning chaos into order, and for her constant calm despite the increasing mental mayhem and expanding girths of our pregnancies! Thanks also to Colinette Yarns Ltd, Sirdar Spinning Ltd, Texere Yarns, Jaegar Handknits and Rowan Yarns for their supply of splendid yarns.

Index